The Financialization of GDP

Gross domestic product (GDP) and other statistics based on national income accounting are ubiquitous but rarely understood today. GDP has been criticized for many reasons, including not reflecting well-being, leaving out the costs of environmental pollution, and not counting unpaid work, but on purely economic terms it has been mostly accepted as an indicator of economic performance. In recent decades, however, GDP has diverged dramatically from economic trends such as employment and median income. This book argues that GDP is flawed even as a narrow economic indicator, and traces the problem to the way financial services are measured.

The first part of the book is a political history of the practice of national accounting from its beginning in the mid-seventeenth century to the present day, and explores how such income estimates were constructed for political reasons. *The Financialization of GDP* presents the practice of estimating national income as a historically and political contingent craft – driven by power and not only theory – culminating in the rise of the financial sector and the concomitant inclusion of financial services in GDP in 1993. The second part of the book focuses on the treatment of financial services in national accounting and develops an adjusted measure of output (final gross domestic product, or FGDP), which treats financial revenues as intermediate inputs (or costs) to the economy as a whole. The final part of the book explores the empirical and policy implications of treating finance as an overall cost to the economy.

This volume shows that the Great Moderation of volatility was a statistical artefact; Okun's Law (relating changes in output and unemployment) never died, and even provides early signs for the Great Recession that analysts using standard GDP did not see. This book is of great interest to those who study political economy and macroeconomics.

Jacob Assa is Economic Affairs Officer at the United Nations, New York. Born and raised in Israel, Jacob attended Hunter College in New York, and has been working at the United Nations since 1999. He received his master's and PhD degrees in economics at the New School for Social Research.

Routledge Advances in Heterodox Economics

Edited by Mark Setterfield
Trinity College, USA
and
Peter Kriesler
University of New South Wales

Over the past two decades, the intellectual agendas of heterodox economists have taken a decidedly pluralist turn. Leading thinkers have begun to move beyond the established paradigms of Austrian, feminist, Institutional-evolutionary, Marxian, Post Keynesian, radical, social, and Sraffian economics – opening up new lines of analysis, criticism, and dialogue among dissenting schools of thought. This cross-fertilization of ideas is creating a new generation of scholarship in which novel combinations of heterodox ideas are being brought to bear on important contemporary and historical problems.

Routledge Advances in Heterodox Economics aims to promote this new scholarship by publishing innovative books in heterodox economic theory, policy, philosophy, intellectual history, institutional history, and pedagogy. Syntheses or critical engagement of two or more heterodox traditions are especially encouraged.

For a full list of titles in this series, please visit www.routledge.com/series/RAHE

25. Advancing the Frontiers of Heterodox Economics
Essays in honor of Frederic S. Lee
Edited by Tae-Hee Jo and Zdravka Todorova

26. Marx, Veblen, and the Foundations of Heterodox Economics
Essays in Honor of John F. Henry
Edited by Tae-Hee Jo and Frederick S. Lee

27. The Problem of Production
A new theory of the firm
Per L. Bylund

28. A New Economic Theory of Public Support for the Arts
Evolution, Veblen and the predatory arts
Arnaldo Barone

29. Varieties of Economic Inequality
Edited by Sebastiano Fadda and Pasquale Tridico

30. Reclaiming Pluralism in Economics
Edited by Jerry Courvisanos, Jamie Doughney and Alex Millmow

31. Policy Implications of Evolutionary and Institutional Economics
Edited by Claudius Gräbner, Torsten Heinrich and Henning Schwardt

32. The Financialization of GDP
Implications for economic theory and policy
Jacob Assa

The Financialization of GDP

Implications for economic theory and policy

Jacob Assa

Routledge
Taylor & Francis Group
LONDON AND NEW YORK

First published 2017 by Routledge

2 Park Square, Milton Park, Abingdon, Oxfordshire OX14 4RN
52 Vanderbilt Avenue, New York, NY 10017

Routledge is an imprint of the Taylor & Francis Group, an informa business

First issued in paperback 2019

British Library Cataloguing in Publication Data
A catalogue record for this book is available from the British Library

Library of Congress Cataloguing in Publication Data
A catalog record has been requested for this book

ISBN: 978-1-138-99983-1 (hbk)
ISBN: 978-0-367-87570-1 (pbk)

Typeset in Times New Roman
by Out of House Publishing

To Shana

Contents

Figures

Tables

Foreword

Brett Christophers

The argument that in recent decades the "advanced" capitalist nations have been experiencing a period of profound "financialization" is now a commonplace in scholarly disciplines ranging from sociology to political economy and from political science to human geography. Companies have allegedly been financialized, succumbing to the singular demands of shareholder-value hegemony. Individuals' everyday lives are also said to have been financialized as they are called upon to become responsible, financially literate, risk-bearing investor-subjects. And perhaps above all else, it is widely argued that capitalism per se, especially in its UK and US variants, has become financialized, with financial activities accounting for a steadily growing share of economy-wide revenues and profits.

In this terrific and challenging book, Jacob Assa forcefully adds his voice to those (e.g. Christophers, 2015) advocating a tempering of this narrative. And he does so in a unique way. The idea that contemporary capitalism represents a form of financialized capitalism is problematic, Assa maintains, because the statistical measure most commonly employed to demonstrate such financialization – gross domestic product, of which finance is estimated to have accounted for an increasing proportional quantum – has *itself* been financialized. Hence: "the financialization of GDP."

But what does Assa mean by this? What he means is that the way in which GDP is calculated has been changed in recent decades in such a way as to boost the relative contribution to GDP that the financial sector is seen to make, regardless of any actual transformation in the underlying economy. He pinpoints two key moments, both related to changes in the United Nations' (UN) internationally observed standard set of recommendations on how to compile measures of economic activity – its System of National Accounts (SNA). First, in 1993, SNA recommended a new treatment of financial intermediation activities that for the first time posited them as explicitly value-adding. Then, in 2008, the range of financial services to be treated as explicitly value-adding was further expanded, beyond simple intermediation. In the process, finance, without necessarily doing anything different, substantively grew its share of GDP, and thus its ostensible productiveness. Assa's point is therefore a profound one: that the crucial abovementioned macroeconomic outcome identified by observers of capitalism – the latter's financialization – is to one extent or another *implicit in the measure used to substantiate it*. The measure is not neutral, or innocent.

Assa is not the first to make this suggestion, although he is one of the clearest, and, importantly, the first to articulate the issue in these specific, arresting, terms: which is to say, in terms of GDP's own financialization. His most distinctive contribution in this book, rather, is to at once recognize the problematic nature of the existing statistical framing and to suggest an alternative approach to GDP measurement.

While Assa does not couch it in these terms, his alternative harks back to the understanding of finance contained in the seminal texts of classical Western political economy – those of Adam Smith, David Ricardo and Karl Marx – wherein finance was conceptualized as non-value-adding. Thus, Assa's preferred metric – final GDP (FGDP) – treats financial activities not as a positive economic output or even (as some historic versions of GDP compilation have done) as value-neutral but instead as an intermediate input – and thus as a net *cost* to the wider economy.

Assa suggests that this alternative treatment of the financial sector potentially helps to resolve some key statistical quandaries within contemporary macroeconomics. One is the much-discussed phenomenon of "jobless growth": the apparent curiosity of periods of economic growth coinciding with flat or declining levels of employment. For Assa, there is no curiosity: according to his FGDP measure, and its converse framing of the finance sector's economic contribution, the economy has not in fact been growing during the periods in question. It is therefore unsurprising that employment levels have not risen either.

To my mind, however, the main contribution of *The Financialization of GDP* lies elsewhere and is explicitly – and unapologetically – political. As Assa makes thoroughly clear, GDP represents an inordinately powerful form of "numerical rhetoric" that encourages and augments particular economic and even social policies. It is crucial not only to how we, as a society, see the world, but to how we – or at least the powerful among us – act on it. Thus the creeping financialization of the official, UN measure of GDP, Assa maintains, has aided and abetted moves to financialize the economic world that official GDP pretends to merely, dispassionately, measure. If this is indeed the case, then Assa's alternative, explicitly *de*financialized, measure of GDP aspires to do precisely the opposite – which is a deeply and bravely political gesture in a world where the political power of the financial sector is beyond dispute. For this, Assa deserves considerable respect, and his book a wide and close reading.

Reference

Christophers, B. (2015). The limits to financialization. *Dialogues in Human Geography*, 5(2), 183–200.

Preface

This book is based on the author's doctoral dissertation at the Economics Department of the New School for Social Research in New York. The inspiration for the research which led to the thesis came from two sources. The historical part of the dissertation was inspired by Brett Christophers' article "Making finance productive" in the journal *Economy and Society* (Christophers, 2011). His view that national accounting – the practice at the basis of computing key macroeconomic statistics such as gross domestic product and national income (NI) – was a techno-political process rather than one of scientific measurement opened up the door for my research on the history of national accounting more generally (that is, beyond the question of how finance has been represented in the accounts over time). As I read several works in the historical literature on national accounting, from Studenski (1958) to Bos (1995), the primary sources cited in this secondary literature all seemed to point in a similar direction. Estimating national income appeared to proceed separately from as well as considerably ahead of economic theory, and to be based first and foremost on quantifying the economic power of nations, classes, or particular policies. Data availability played a part, as did bits and pieces of theory, but given the large leeway available in constructing these complex estimates (unlike the strict definitions of measuring, say, the unemployment rate), theory and data played a secondary and passive role vis-à-vis the political elements. This became harder to uncover in postwar national accounting, as governments took over the role of compilers from individuals, and increasing standardization occurred, but the undercurrents of power and policy were still there in the 2008 revision of the System of National Accounts, as they had been in William Petty's first estimate in 1665.

A second inspiration, in a form of a paper by Deepankar Basu and Duncan Foley in the *Cambridge Journal of Economics* (Basu and Foley, 2013), inspired the empirical and analytical second half of this book.

While Basu and Foley's main focus was the change in the relationship between real output and employment, one of their innovations was the introduction of several alternative measures of output, including narrow measured value added (NMVA). This measure differs from standard value added (which is one of the three methods for calculating GDP) in that it excludes all industries where output is imputed (based on net income) rather than directly measured. The sectors omitted in constructing NMVA are the government, finance, insurance and real estate (FIRE), other services and the rest of the world. Basu and Foley show an improved correlation between employment and NMVA as compared with NI or GDP, resulting from their omissions of imputations for the industries mentioned above.

My key interest in building on this insight was to see whether the correlation can be even further improved by treating the value added of the FIRE sector as an intermediate input (or economic cost) rather than an output, that is – by assigning a negative sign to it in the accounts instead of a positive sign (as in GDP) or dropping it altogether (as in NMVA). The result, final GDP (FGDP), performed better on several levels. Its correlation with employment levels in the United States from 1970 to the most recent period was indeed higher than that of either NMVA or GDP; furthermore, when used for in-sample forecasting, FGDP predicted earlier and more accurately the drop in employment (and aggregate demand) that signaled the Great Recession; and FGDP also shed light on several apparent empirical puzzles that have been debated in the macroeconomic literature recently. The breakdown of Okun's Law, the Great Moderation, and the decoupling of growth from employment (noted in terms such as "jobless growth") all turned out to be statistical artefacts contingent on GDP's treatment of the FIRE sector as value-adding. Seen through the lens of FGDP (which implies that the FIRE sector is value-reducing), Okun's Law holds, volatility in output is greater than ever, and a trend of secular stagnation is revealed once the smoothing effect of treating financial revenues as output is reversed.

Acknowledgments

This book is based on the author's doctoral dissertation in economics at the New School for Social Research, defended in February 2015. I would like to thank the dissertation committee, first and foremost Professor Duncan Foley, whose 2013 paper with Deepankar Basu in the *Cambridge Journal of Economics* inspired my research in this field, and who guided the first year of work. Professor Paulo dos Santos chaired the dissertation committee and provided valuable comments and perspectives on the changing nature of banking. I am especially grateful to Professor Mark Setterfield, who also served on the committee, and who suggested submitting a book proposal to Routledge based on the dissertation. His valuable comments during the processes of thesis writing and revising, proposal submission, and title choice for the book were indispensable for the completion of this project. Finally, I am grateful to Brett Christophers, both for his inspiring work on the representation of finance and banking in national accounts and for writing the foreword to this book.

I would like to further thank Mr. Andrew Humphries and Ms. Laura Johnson at Routledge for their support during the publication process, as well as two anonymous reviewers for their useful comments on the initial book proposal.

Introduction
The economic problem with GDP

> So in summary, Your Majesty, the failure to foresee the timing, extent and severity of the crisis and to head it off, while it had many causes, was principally a failure of the collective imagination of many bright people, both in this country and internationally, to understand the risks to the system as a whole.
>
> (Letter from the British Academy to Queen Elizabeth II, July 22, 2009)

As the quote above suggests, the economics profession as a whole did not see the financial crisis of 2007–2008 coming (with a few notable exceptions).[1] While many reasons have been offered for this failure – including over-specialization, too much reliance on mathematical models, and unrealistic assumptions in these models – this book suggests that the headline data themselves were (and still are) part of the problem.[2]

The few exceptions to the above-mentioned professional blind spot lend credence to this idea, since they had voiced their early warnings and concerns using indicators beyond GDP to make their point. Godley and Wray (1999) looked at the "fiscal ratio" – government spending divided by the average rate of taxation – and compared it to GDP to derive a measure of fiscal stance (e.g. if the fiscal ratio is greater than GDP, this will stimulate aggregate demand), and then extended the analysis using a "trade ratio" (total exports and international transfers divided by the average propensity to import) and its derived trade stance. Godley (2001) combined these two measures to derive an "augmented fiscal stance," and then tracked its divergence from GDP starting in the early 1990s. He then supplemented this analysis with calculations of the private sector's financial balance. Godley (2000) also used the net borrowing and saving of several developed countries (compiled from National Income and Product Accounts (NIPA), flow of funds and IMF data) to warn of "horrendous" results in the form of a "severe recession" if a recovery of private net savings were to occur quickly. Palley (2002) highlighted the importance of household debt using data on such debt by income groups from the Federal Reserve 1998 Survey of Consumer Finances.

What all these visionary papers have in common (besides standing out in a crowd at a time of market euphoria) is their reliance on indicators other than GDP (often based on data from outside the core NIPA framework) to make their point, and their use of these data series either aside from GDP, in proportion to GDP, or – most interestingly for our purposes – side by side with, and diverging from, GDP.

The implication of this characteristic of the analyses of impending crisis – their need to go beyond GDP in order to warn that not all is as rosy as it seems – adds to increasing dissatisfaction with this aggregate from two other angles. GDP has diverged dramatically from employment in recent decades, as witnessed by the phenomena of jobless recoveries and severe job-loss downturns (Basu and Foley, 2013). Examples of these apparent anomalies include the two business cycles in the US before the 2007 crisis (when employment increased much more slowly compared with GDP than standard models predicted), and the downturn in 2009 (when GDP fell far less than models would predict based on the increase in the rate of unemployment). GDP has also been criticized for not accurately reflecting people's perceptions of their standard of living. In February 2008, former French president Nicolas Sarkozy formed the Commission on the Measurement of Economic Performance and Social Progress, chaired by Joseph Stiglitz (with Amartya Sen as advisor and Jean Paul Fitoussi as coordinator). The purpose of the Commission was to look into the "marked distance between standard measures of important socio-economic variables like economic growth, inflation, unemployment, etc. and widespread perceptions," which lead, inter alia, to undermining of public trust in official statistics (Stiglitz, 2009, and see Chapter 2).

It is important to note that the discussion here does not relate to other, extra-economic critiques of GDP, such as its inability to indicate welfare (e.g. those by Simon Kuznets, Amartya Sen, the Human Development Index, and the Nordhaus-Tobin view), its omission of the environmental costs and consequences of economic activity, or the fact that care work is not counted as production in GDP. Thus the critique of GDP in this book is on purely economic grounds, that is to say, GDP fails to provide a reasonably accurate measure of economic activity even by its own definition as the sum of all goods and services produced in an economy at a given time and place.

In order to understand why this is the case, one needs to look at the issue from several angles. Chapter 1 discusses why GDP is different and far more complex than most other economic indicators (e.g. the unemployment rate or the consumer price index). This complexity is partly due to the fact that GDP, unlike narrower indicators, is by design broad enough to capture the workings of an entire economy rather than just one aspect of it. It is also due, however, to the way national accounting has developed over centuries and across countries. Chapter 2 therefore reviews both the historical and critical literatures on national accounting, and finds that while the former is technocratic in nature (i.e. focusing on changes in scope, statistical sources, and methods used), the latter often lacks the historical basis of critiquing GDP. The resulting gap analysis thus argues for a combined approach of historically informed assessment of GDP's shortcomings.

Chapter 3 fills the gap by presenting a history of national income estimates which is fundamentally different than other histories provided to date. While most narratives of the development of national accounting are not only technocratic but also teleological (that is, they trace a constant process of improvement leading to the current measures), the account provided here is a political history of national accounting. In each period, dominant or dissenting voices (in different countries, classes, and industries) influenced the measurement of aggregate economic activity based on their desired economic policies and representations of economic power. Rather than a linear path of technical improvement, the history of national accounting thus reveals a path of uneven and contested development, pulled in different directions by competing interests. The most recent inflection point in this history is the rise of the financial sector, and the impact of its power on the 1993 and 2008 revisions of the System of National Accounts, the international standards for calculating GDP.

These new ways of measuring economic activity present finance, real estate and insurance (FIRE) as contributing directly (and in some economies, such as the US and the UK, enormously) to output. Chapter 4 therefore focuses in depth on the role of the FIRE sector in the deterioration in GDP's performance, tracing the particular history of FIRE's representation in national accounting since 1953. Finance was initially considered to have a negligible or even negative contribution to economic output, but by the end of the Cold War its representation in the national accounts has been transformed into a sector which not only positively contributes to production but apparently does so with far less labor input than others (thus appearing as one of the most productive industries). The analysis then challenges this spurious productivity miracle by examining whether finance and related industries (producing and trading assets rather than goods and services) create direct use-value and, therefore, can be considered as having a final output. Based on both theoretical and empirical arguments, an adjustment to GDP is presented wherein the FIRE sectors are instead accounted for as intermediate inputs or costs in the production of all other goods and services. While seemingly radical, this treatment is similar to both SNA 53 and SNA 68 in terms of presenting finance as an input of other industries, rather than a (final) output. The resulting adjusted aggregate (final GDP or FGDP) is shown to have far better correlation with measures of median income and employment (and thus aggregate demand) than GDP. Since the analysis is carried out using the output (value added) approach, the appendix to Chapter 4 contains technical details on the reconciliation of the adjusted output aggregate to the expenditure and income approach as well.

Chapter 5 examines the theoretical and policy implications of the financialization of GDP by comparing it with FGDP, its definancialized version. FGDP – GDP adjusted for the economic cost of finance (accounted for as an intermediate input or a tax) – sheds light on several important macroeconomic empirical puzzles. The so-called Great Moderation of output volatility is shown to be a statistical artefact due to the smoothing effect of including financial revenues as output, in the absence of which output is far more volatile. GDP also performs far worse than FGDP as a leading and forecasting indicator and thus helps explain why analysts using the former did not see the coming of the Great Recession. Rumors of the demise of Okun's Law – which relates changes in output to changes in unemployment – appear to have been exaggerated, since after adjusting GDP for the economic cost of finance the relationship seems alive and well.

Chapter 6 examines the distributional implications of looking at the economy through the lens of FGDP rather than GDP. By treating financial revenues as a cost or tax, FGDP allows us to see their role as demand leakages which weaken the multiplier, give investment and government spending a more prominent role in expenditure vis-à-vis consumption, and locate the lion's share of income in wages rather than profits (since much of what is counted as profits in GDP are mere financial transfers).

The dramatic political economy implications of these findings are discussed in the conclusion, which also assesses what this all means for the economics profession. Correcting our measure of economic output allows us to reintegrate our theoretical and policy views, which are sometimes at odds when it comes to mainstream-trained but liberally minded economists (such as Paul Krugman). If finance indeed is a drag on the economy, and using FGDP lens to expose the secular stagnation hidden under its smoothing effect on GDP, there is no tradeoff between growth and equity, since controlling the socially extractive FIRE sectors, supporting households and wage-earners, and promoting public and private investment are all economically beneficial. It thus makes more sense to bail out the real job creators (wage-earners) rather than the banks.

Notes

1 See Galbraith, J. K. (2009). Who Are These Economists, Anyway? *Thought & Action*, Fall, for a useful summary, including a typology of exceptions by school of thought (radical, bubble-detectors, Keynesians, the Minsky school, and institutionalists).

2 Some followers of Minsky have done work in non-linear dynamics (Albin, 1998, Rosser *et al.*, 2011 and Chen, 2010) – a concept excluded a priori from mainstream models – pursuing an important line of work given that crises are highly non-linear effects of "catastrophes."

1 The ubiquity, importance, and uniqueness of national accounting

John Maynard Keynes famously foresaw "a new era of 'Joy through Statistics'" as his contemporaries began moving beyond theoretical economics and getting involved in applied empirical work (Moggridge, 1976, quoted in Stone, 1978). Looking back from the second decade of the twenty-first century, it appears that Keynes was spectacularly right. Statistics are ubiquitous in many areas of modern life, including political and opinion polls, sports statistics, demographic trends, and, perhaps more than any other type, economic data.

The growth rate of gross domestic product, the level and changes of the rate of unemployment, the inflation rate (as measured by changes in the Consumer Price Index – CPI), and other key macroeconomic figures appear daily in the media. They have the potential to shake markets, affect government policies and corporate strategies, and – increasingly – determine election results. Ratios using GDP in their denominator are used in international agreements, multilateral treaties, and various conditionalities. The Annex to the Maastricht Treaty of 1992 – which created the European Union (EU) as well as its single currency, the Euro – stipulated maxima of 60 percent for the debt-to-GDP ratio and 3 percent for the deficit-to-GDP ratio as admission criteria. Public debt as a percentage of GDP is also a frequently used criterion for the imposition of austerity measures on countries, either by external lenders (such as the EU or the International Monetary Fund – IMF) or internally by government edict (Poland's Public Finance Act, for example, triggers an automatic freezing of the country's proportion of deficit to budget revenues when the debt-to-GDP ratio exceeds 50 percent).

Nor is this concern with economic headline numbers restricted to policy circles. The recent academic controversy surrounding a 2010 paper by Reinhart and Rogoff is a case in point. The paper argued that gross public debt in excess of 90 percent of GDP was associated with "notably lower rates of growth" (Reinhart and Rogoff 2010). This idea was criticized in a 2013 paper by Herndon *et al.* and fueled a furious debate in the op-ed section of *The New York Times*. While some of the controversy had to do with calculation errors in the dataset used as the basis for the 2010 paper, the larger question emerging from this involves the centrality of headline macroeconomic data as a basis for supporting economic policies, both nationally and internationally. Paul Krugman made this point succinctly in the same newspaper: "Austerity enthusiasts trumpeted that supposed 90 percent tipping point as a proven fact and a reason to slash government spending even in the face of mass unemployment" (Krugman, 2013). This certainly casts doubt on the familiar notion of evidence-based policy. But coding errors aside, how objective or neutral is the evidence to start with?

The frequent and high-profile attention and emphasis given to GDP and other national accounting figures have stimulated growing interest in the way such "data" are calculated (the inverted commas betray one of the key points made in this book, i.e. that national accounts aggregates are not *given* by simple measurement or statistical sampling, as the Latin origin of the word – *datum* – would imply, but are rather *constructed* in a complex manner). Unlike other macroeconomic statistics such as the unemployment rate, the national accounts are intricate systems, combining hundreds of data items from multiple sources, and using a variety of assumptions, extrapolations, and imputations to arrive at the headline numbers.

This makes national accounting unique. In a way, the art of national accounting is more akin to that of economic modeling than to the far more straightforward statistical processes involved in calculating other macroeconomic indicators. A simple example would suffice to illustrate this contrast. The US Bureau of Labor Statistics (BLS) defines the unemployed as those who "do not have a job, have actively looked for work in the prior 4 weeks, and are currently available for work" (BLS website). The entire methodology, including a description of data sources and several examples for calculating the unemployment rate, is covered in nine pages. By contrast, the US Bureau of Economic Analysis (BEA) does not even attempt a short definition of GDP or national accounts on its website, instead providing a separate section for "Methodologies." In addition to several primers and introductory papers on the subject, the main document in this methodological section – *Concepts and Methods of the U.S. National Income and Product Accounts* – is 318 pages long (not including Chapters 11 and 12, which are listed separately). The equivalent current international standard, the *System of National Accounts 2008* (SNA 2008), is more than twice as thick with 722 pages. SNA 1993 was even bigger, at 838 pages, compared with 253 and 57 pages for SNA 1968 and SNA 1953, respectively (a trend constituting a methodological inflation of sorts over the past half a century).

Thus it becomes clear that national accounts are not regular economic statistics by any means, if they can be considered statistics at all. In fact, national accounting uses statistics from various sources as inputs, which, through a combination of identities, accounting rules, pieces of economic theory, and assumptions (as well as increasingly more imputations where certain variables cannot be measured directly), are transformed to arrive at the final estimates. A recent paper by the top national accountants in the US describes part of this statistical alchemy:

> In the United States, the GDP and the national accounts estimates are fundamentally based on detailed economic census data and other information that is available only once every five years. The challenge lies in developing a framework and methods that take these economic census data and combine them using a mosaic of monthly, quarterly, and annual economic indicators to produce quarterly and annual GDP estimates. For example, one problem is that the other economic indicators that are used to extrapolate GDP in between the five-year economic census data – such as retail sales, housing starts, and manufacturers' shipments of capital goods – are often collected for purposes other than estimating GDP and may embody definitions that differ from those used in the national accounts. Another problem is some data are simply not available for the earlier estimates. For the initial monthly estimates of quarterly GDP, data on about 25 percent of GDP – especially in the service sector – are not available, and so these sectors of the economy are estimated based on past trends and whatever related data are available. For example, estimates of consumer spending for electricity and gas are extrapolated using past heating and cooling degree data and the actual temperatures, while spending for medical care, education, and welfare services are extrapolated using employment, hours, and earnings data for these sectors from the Bureau of Labor Statistics.
>
> (Landefeld *et al.*, 2008)

In addition to extrapolations due to data availability problems, many crucial decisions need to be made regarding what should or should not be included in GDP. Financial services, for example, used to be excluded based on the convention that interest payments (financial firms' main input and output) were merely transfers, but this changed in recent decades as financial intermediation crossed the production boundary and became defined as a productive activity. Even for items that are included in GDP there are some implicit transactions that are imputed. While the market value of fee-based financial services can be readily measured, the value added of those not provided for a fee cannot, and is imputed on the basis of interest differentials between loans and deposits. Another example is the value added of owner-occupied dwellings, imputed based on the rent that their owner would have to pay otherwise.

All of these processes require a lot of ingenuity, but also leave plenty of room for maneuver, a fact that is evident throughout the history of national accounting estimates around the world and over the centuries. One current example of this flexibility is the recent revision in the BEA methodology for the second-quarter estimates of US GDP in 2013. The new definition includes research and development as well as original entertainment works as part of fixed investment – items that formerly were excluded since they were considered to be intermediate inputs in the production process (and also due to conceptual difficulties with their ownership and durability). This adjustment has added $560 billion to total output (more than the entire GDP of Sweden), and has increased the US's GDP to $16.2 trillion, conveniently "reinforcing America's status as the world's largest economy and opening up a bit more breathing space over fast-closing China" (Economist Intelligence Unit, 2013). Nor is the US the only country to make this change. Canada had done the same in 2012 and Australia as early as 2009, at the time "leapfrogging Canada in the OECD's country rankings of GDP per person" (*The Economist*, 2013, 64). This economic race echoes the concerns of seventeenth-century national accounts pioneers such as William Petty and Gregory King with inter-country comparisons of economic strength and position. As we shall see below, this is not a coincidence.

Given both the importance and complexity of constructing as well as adjusting the content and scope of national accounts, it becomes critical to ask: what drives the evolution of these intricate systems in different periods and countries, and what explains the differences (and, later, revisions) between the various resulting structures? That is the main research question of the next two chapters of this book. Received histories of national accounts take a technocratic approach to the topic, explaining the development of these estimates as a statistical exercise informed by economic theory and available data. The next chapter proposes an alternative hypothesis – power drives measurement – which views national income estimates as exercises in numerical rhetoric. A key force in shaping national accounting has been national economic policy, not merely as a general, passive end-use of national accounts but as an influence shaping the structure, content, and revision of different systems to support particular policies advocated by their authors, whether individual or institutional. This was as true in 2014 as it was in the seventeenth century.

2 National accounting as a historically and politically contingent art

> It is just as foolish to fancy that any philosophy can transcend its present world, as that an individual could leap out of his time or jump over Rhodes.
>
> (Georg Wilhelm Friedrich Hegel, Preface to *The Philosophy of Right*, 1821)

One part of the literature on national accounting consists of histories, either in one country or globally, written in a mostly descriptive style. Another literature strand consists of political economy critiques of (current) national accounting standards, based on their inclusion or exclusion of certain categories of economic activities. The problem with these two sub-literatures is that while the first is historical but not critical (assuming overall progress and improvement through time), the second is critical but a-historical, touching only briefly (if at all) on previous systems and thus not investigating how the issues it critiques came about in the first place. Figure 2.1 visualizes this problem.[1]

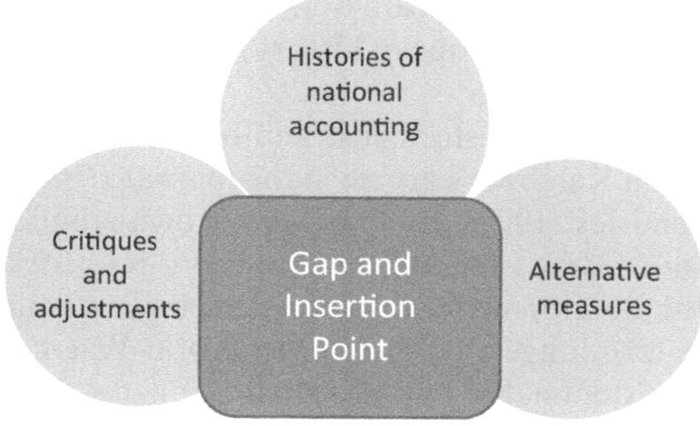

Figure 2.1 Three sub-literatures on national accounting, their gap, and the proposed contribution to the literature

2.1 Technocratic histories of national income estimates

Works in the historical literature on national accounts provide plenty of historical and technical detail, but seem to assume overall progress (albeit occasionally interrupted) in the development of national accounting systems. Such histories of national income estimates and accounting impose a twentieth-century utilitarian view – that the accounts are based on economic theory and attempt to measure output and productivity – on a 400-year-old tradition which they do not fully understand.

The classic work in this strand of literature is Studenski's *The Income of Nations* (1958). Although treating concepts and methodology as well as presenting contemporary accounts for a selected group of countries, the book contains (and is most cited for) a detailed history of estimates of national income from the mid-seventeenth century to the 1950s, comprising its first ten chapters. Studenski concludes this historical part of the book with a section entitled "Forces that influenced the development of the past three hundred years" (158–160). Of the eleven factors listed, the top three are individual scholars' initiative and interest, advances in economic theory, and external events such as severe economic crises, wars, and revolutions.

While this is certainly a reasonable list of factors, all of which may have contributed at some level to motivating the development of national accounting, there is no clear thread connecting these seemingly isolated forces, other than a general emphasis on these factors as the most important in the overall history of national accounting. As we will see, even this emphasis is misguided, since individual initiative and economic theory both flourished in periods and places where no significant or original efforts to estimate national income were observed, while wars, revolutions, and severe economic crises – viewed in isolation – are too frequent and ubiquitous (particularly in European history) to serve as an explanatory factor of any power.

Another work in the historical strand of the national accounting literature is John Kendrick's article in the journal *History of Political Economy* (Kendrick, 1970). By the author's own admission, the first part of the piece draws heavily on Studenski. Kendrick divides the history of the development of national income accounts into two main phases. The longest period, up to World War I, is characterized by him as dominated by individual estimates driven primarily by intellectual curiosity coupled with 'nationalism' – "the desire to compare the economic performances of rival nations and the need to build quantitative bases for analysis of the effects of proposed tax policies and other policies meant to strengthen and reform national economies" (284).

The second phase in Kendrick's history begins in the 1920s, with progress accelerating due to the heightened need of national governments for better quantitative evidence in the wake of the Great Depression, World War II, and the Cold War. Other motivating factors mentioned are the needs of reconstruction and economic development, theories of demand and employment, and new theories of economic growth. All this resulted in "[t]he invention of the structure of interlocking sets of sector accounts, and the independent formulation of input–output and flow-of-funds accounts, and sector balance sheets capable of integration with the basic production accounts" (ibid., 285). The main idea in this history is that "economic accounts are a continually evolving structure and body of statistics," with changes and improvements – both past and future – reflecting "interacting dynamic changes in society and the economy, in concepts and economic theories, in data collection and processing, and in methodologies of estimation and analysis" (ibid., 315). Kendrick thus reflects the technocratic view of the development of national accounting in this literature – a secular progress over time, mirroring the progress of economic theory as well as of statistical methods, with each subsequent version superseding, rather than merely replacing, all others.

Kendrick's student at George Washington University, Carol Carson, wrote her PhD dissertation on the history of national accounts in the US under his guidance in 1971. The thesis served as the basis for her paper "The history of the United States national income and product accounts: the development of an analytical tool" (Carson, 1975). As its title suggests, the paper focuses on the US, and begins by briefly reviewing the early history of national income estimates there. It then discusses the estimates made by the Department of Commerce in response to the Great Depression, the use of national accounts during World War II, and the postwar consolidation of the national income and product accounts. While providing plenty of detail on the economists and agencies involved, as well as the technical evolution of the accounts, the assumption in this paper is similar to that of Kendrick – an ongoing refinement of a tool for macroeconomic analysis.

A similar description of the development of national accounts, in this case for Britain (though only for the period 1895–1941), is provided in Tily (2009). The paper's main goals as stated by its author are to clarify John Maynard Keynes's role in the development of national accounts, as well as to showcase the contribution of lesser-known figures of the time, such as Alfred Flux, Arthur Bowley, Josiah Stamp, and Colin Clark. Tily challenges the common wisdom that it was Keynes and his theories that provided the first impetus to the development of national accounting in 1930s Britain, arguing that earlier developments – such as Alfred Marshall's elaboration of national income concepts, as well as the 1907 Census of Production – were among the original drivers of this process. Keynes's multifaceted role as a "user, supporter and producer of economic statistics" is also explored in detail (Tily, 2009, 332). According to Tily, economic theory, especially of the Keynesian variety (though not limited to or even beginning with Keynes himself), was the most important factor in the history of national accounting. For example, in Tily's view, "it was the discovery of the multiplier that gave the greatest impetus to developments of National Accounts in the 1930s in both the U.K. and U.S." (ibid., 343).

The next two pieces in the historical strand of the literature on national accounting are once more global in scope. A paper by Dutch statistician and national accountant Frits Bos, *The History of National Accounting* (1992), traces the historical roots of the 1968 System of National Accounts (SNA 68) standard, which was used by most countries at the time. Bos builds on the work of Studenski and Kendrick cited above, but uses a three-phased approach to his history. The first period in Bos's framework is one of "national accounting as a free enterprise," extending from the seventeenth century to the 1930s. The second period consists of the "revolutionary decades" of the 1930s and 1940s, which witnessed "a revitalization of discussion on basic national accounting concepts, three innovations in economic theory which were of direct importance to national accounting (input–output analysis, econometric modelling of the national economy and the Keynesian revolution) and the birth of the first [official] national accounting systems" (Bos, 1992, 3). Third and final is the period of international guidelines beginning in 1947 and culminating in the 1968 SNA.

While noting the gradual increase in the number of estimates from the end of the seventeenth century to the early twentieth, Bos nonetheless concludes that "[s]ubstantial progress in national accounting as an applied science was mostly absent until the 1930s and 1940s" (ibid., 27). For Bos, as for Kendrick and Tily, the key influence on national accounting was theoretical – Keynesian analysis, input–output tables, and econometric modeling. He does point out the "applied and policy-oriented nature" of the modern accounts, "as the general circumstances of crisis and war (preparations and recovery) urgently demanded new and practical tools for economic policy" (ibid.). Notwithstanding this reference to policy, however,

Bos's focus is on innovations and improvements in national accounts, mostly driven by theory, with policy playing a passive role on the demand side, so to speak, for national accounting data (that is, as a final use rather than a direct influence on the path of development of the accounts). Bos elaborated his 1992 paper into a PhD dissertation in 2006 entitled *The National Accounts as a Tool for Analysis and Policy: Past, Present and Future*. While this work gives much more detail than his previous paper and consists of more than 300 pages, the same philosophy applies to this historical account, namely, it is seen as a technical progression from "incidental estimates to a universal tool for analysis and policy" (Bos, 2006, 7).

The broadest contribution to the historical literature on national accounts to date is André Vanoli's *History of National Accounting* (2005). Vanoli considers national accounting to be "a product of the 20th century," and views the preceding 250 years of estimates as mainly a pre-history of the practice (albeit an impressive one), where "[e]stimates were intermittent and extended slowly" (Vanoli, 2008, 2). Instead, the main factors spurring the development of national accounts for Vanoli are "the Great Depression, the Second World War and the subsequent period of recovery and economic growth" (ibid.). He also puts emphasis on the theoretical achievements of Keynes, Grüning, and Leontief, as well as on the idea of using an accounting approach to national income, similar to business accounting, as key factors leading to improvement in the estimates. While during World War II the focus was on war financing, the ensuing postwar period witnessed a "golden age" of national accounting (ibid., 3):

> Economic reconstruction and growth policies, the large increase in the economic role of government and the welfare state, the extension of international cooperation (for example, the Marshall Plan and, later, the Common Market in Europe), with the consequent emphasis on measuring of the rate of growth, led to a great demand for national accounts. This comprised the requirements of Keynesian macroeconomic demand management for short-term economic budget forecasts and longer-term projections needed for various types of indicative planning (the latter being particularly important in France). The development of econometric techniques and national accounts estimates reinforced each other. This trend towards greater use of national accounting data was general, even though the economies involved ranged from basically liberal economies such as the United States to more controlled economies such as France, the Netherlands and Norway.

Vanoli continues with a discussion of the international harmonization of national accounts culminating in the 1968 SNA. The mid-1970s saw a period of challenges and, since 1980, "after the supply shocks of the 1970s and the decreasing role played by macro econometric models, national accounting has no longer been supported by the Keynesian paradigm" (ibid., 7). By the 1993 SNA, the accounting framework included balance sheets, a revaluation account for holding gains and losses, and some accounting for intangible capital formation. "Nearly full integration was achieved between the SNA and the International Monetary Fund manuals (Balance of Payments, Government Finance Statistics, Monetary and Financial Statistics)" (ibid.), making the accounts more universal in scope. Vanoli also admits to remaining difficulties, including the fact that GDP is not a welfare indicator, and discusses some extensions to the traditional accounts (such as the UN's 1993 *Handbook on Integrated Environmental and Economic Accounting*). He concludes by observing that "[t]ensions between social concerns, theoretical issues and observation constraints of actual economies are increasingly at stake" (ibid., 9).

Vanoli was himself intimately involved with the practice of national accounting, having worked at the French Central Statistical Office (INSEE) as director of national accounts, as well as serving as one of the main authors of SNA 1993. His book is thus an expert-level sequel to Studenski's much older classic, and fills the gap left after the latter's 1958 book. This strength, however, is also the work's weakness, since it epitomizes the technocratic notion of continued progress in the history of national accounting, linking economic theories to the measurement of the economy in a technical but non-critical way. Vanoli's perspective is perhaps the clearest example of the Whig historical approach to national accounting which pervades some of the other works in this field.[2]

Finally, a recent and very interesting contribution to the history of national accounts literature is a doctoral dissertation by Mitra-Kahn (2011). The work questions the very point of criticizing GDP as an indicator of economic performance, claiming that it is rather a definition of the economy. It uses primary sources to track this changing definition over time, and argues that "GDP is simply the most recent consensus definition of the economy in a long history of definitions against which policy makers evaluate their impact and economists frame their theories" (Mitra-Kahn, 2011). Once again, however, this point of view focuses on the theoretical conception of the economy, and relegates other factors to a passive role vis-à-vis the accounts, which appear to yield objective data used for theoretical and policy-making purposes.

2.2 GDP ex machina: political economy critiques of national accounts

The second part of the literature on national accounts consists of political economy critiques of current national accounting systems and standards, focusing on specific issues, and offering alternatives. Research in this vein addresses the rationale (or lack thereof) for the inclusion or exclusion of various components in the accounts – unpaid domestic work, financial intermediation, public consumption (such as military expenditures), environmental inputs and impacts, etc. While these works are clearly critical of the latest national accounting systems, they more often than not neglect to look at the overall historical trend, thus failing to explore exactly how and why the accounts they critique came to be that way. The main focus is on economic thought, whether a critique of neoclassical theory or an advocacy of an alternative (classical, Marxian, feminist, etc.) as a basis for reforming the accounts. The following is a brief summary of key contributions in this literature.[3]

One attempt to extend the coverage of GDP, from a supply-side and Austrian perspective, was presented in Mark Skousen's book *The Structure of Production* (1990). The proposed concept of Gross Output (GO) is broader than that of GDP, in that it attempts to measure the "make" economy rather than the "use" economy. This is done by including spending at all stages of the production process, rather than just final output as in GDP. GO thus includes a large component of business-to-business transactions, which are excluded from GDP based on their status as intermediate inputs. The BEA began estimating GO in the first quarter of 2014, showing a series going back to 2005.

By contrast, Shaikh and Tonak's book (1994) positions their critique of modern national accounts as different from those of orthodox economists. While the latter seek to extend or improve the coverage of the accounts, the former question the very definition of production embodied in them. They consider military, police, trading, and administrative activities to be "really forms of social consumption, not production" (Shaikh and Tonak, 1994, 2). This distinction harks back to the classical political economists, and was later blurred by neoclassical theory (even Keynesian economics did not deviate from the mainstream on this issue). Shaikh and Tonak extend another distinction – the one between outcome and output (evident in the case of personal consumption) – to social consumption as well. The outcome of all such activities is "protection, distribution, [or] administration" rather than the production of new wealth (ibid.). The argument thus pits classical vs. neoclassical economic theories as the main determining factor in the development of the accounts.

The highest-profile work on the shortcomings of GDP is the Report by the Commission on the Measurement of Economic Performance and Social Progress (2010), also known as the Stiglitz Commission after its chair (Amartya Sen was its chair advisor and Jean Paul Fitoussi its coordinator). The political weight of the report was partly due to its promotion by then-president of France, Nicolas Sarkozy, who also wrote a forward to a book version of it, *Mismeasuring Our Lives: Why GDP Doesn't Add Up* (Stiglitz *et al.*, 2010). The report questions the suitability of GDP as a well-being indicator on three levels – classical GDP issues, quality of life, and sustainable development and environment. In addition to these particular critiques and suggestions to overcome them, the authors make an important observation that usually escapes even astute critics of standard national accounting measures:

> [T]here often seems to be a marked distance between standard measures of important socio economic variables like economic growth, inflation, unemployment, etc. and widespread perceptions. The standard measures may suggest, for instance, that there is less inflation or more growth than individuals perceive to be the case, and the gap is so large and so universal that it cannot be explained by reference to money illusion or to human psychology. In some countries, this gap has undermined confidence in official statistics (for example, in France and in the United Kingdom, only one third of citizens trust official figures, and these countries are not exceptions), with a clear impact on the way in which public discourse about the conditions of the economy and necessary policies takes place.
>
> (Stiglitz *et al.*, 2010)

Despite this important acknowledgment, the report suffers from the same problem evident in other works in this literature, namely, a focus on the latest, existing system without reference to the way it has developed historically. This has the effect of presenting GDP as *deus ex machina*, something imperfect appearing out of thin air, which must now be improved. It is much harder, however, to change such politically sensitive standards without understanding what powerful forces shaped them in the first place.

Finally, a recent book (co-authored by a participant in the above-mentioned Commission) surveys various attempts to go beyond GDP.

Fleurbaey and Blanchet (2013) use a theory-based framework to make sense of the "growing mountain of initiatives, indicators and methodologies" proposed as alternatives to GDP. One merit of this book is the authors' acknowledgment that national accounting is value-laden, and not merely a technical exercise. Their attempts to extend the debate beyond theory, however, are limited to the realms of philosophy and morals, thus shying away from a more political discussion of the accounts.

2.3 Theory is not enough

The technocratic approach to the history of national accounting described above is not only historically inaccurate, it also leaves four questions unanswered if we accept its emphasis on economic theory as a key explanatory variable. The history of economic thought alone cannot explain the following riddles:

Question 1: *Why did national income measurement first appear in the middle of the seventeenth century, rather than earlier or later? And why did this practice begin in England and France, while in other countries, for example Germany and Italy, it only began towards the end of the nineteenth century?*

Economic theory is not a useful answer here, since the first estimates of national income precede Adam Smith and even the Physiocrats by nearly a century (Smith's *Wealth of Nations* was published in 1776, and Quesnay's *Tableau Economique* in 1758, compared with Petty's 1665 book *Political Arithmetick*, which contained the first known estimate of national income). Economic theory thus lagged national income estimates by almost a century.

Question 2: *Why have there been comparatively few estimates between the late seventeenth century and the early twentieth century?*

This is indeed a mystery, as the period in question saw the rise of the classical political economists, including Adam Smith, David Ricardo, John Stuart Mill and Karl Marx (not to mention Alfred Marshall or the marginalists). Their seminal and original work in economic theory and political economy, however, was clearly not sufficient to generate the kind of empirical curiosity evident in either the seventeenth or the twentieth centuries.

Question 3: *What caused the revival of national accounting in the 1920s and 1930s?*

Economic theory is once more insufficient as an explanatory variable here. Keynes's revolutionary *General Theory* was published in 1936, but government estimates of national income already appeared in 1921 (NBER), 1926 (Popov in the USSR), 1932 (Germany; Clark in the UK), 1933 (the Netherlands; Kuznets in the US), and 1934 (The Brookings Institute).

Question 4: *Why was there such a long gap between the 1968 SNA and the 1993 SNA?*

While the 1960s and 1970s saw significant changes in economic theory – monetarism, new classical economics, and the anti-Keynesian revolution – no revision was made to the international standard – the System of National Accounts – until the early 1990s. Once again that something else must have been at play.

Notes

1 The figure also shows a third strand of research – alternative measures. This category includes works that do not attempt to adjust GDP but rather present completely different measures of well-being, such as the Human Development Index (HDI), the Happy Life Index, the Millennium Development Goals (MDGs), etc. Fleurbaey and Blanchet (2013) provide a comprehensive survey. As mentioned in Chapter 1, however, the focus of this book is on the *economic* problem with GDP.

2 The "Whig" historical approach has been applied to other fields in economics, and consists of the tendency "to emphasize certain principles of progress in the past and to produce a story which is the ratification if not the glorification of the present" (Butterfield, 1931). When it comes to histories of national income estimates and accounting, this trend involves imposing a twentieth-century view of the accounts as measures of output and productivity on a 400-year-old tradition which is far more complex and diverse than this simplification suggests.

3 The discussion here covers heterodox critiques. For mainstream points of view, Eisner (1988) provides a useful survey.

3 Policy-based evidence

A political history of national accounts

> The philosophers have only interpreted the world, in various ways; the point is to change it.
>
> (Karl Marx, Theses on Feuerbach, # 11, 1845)

3.1 Beyond economic theory: political arithmetic as numerical rhetoric

It thus becomes our task to propose an alternative hypothesis for answering the key research question in the first part of this book, namely, what has been the main driving force behind the evolution of these complex systems in different periods and countries, and what explains the differences between the various resulting structures?

In the context of the evolution of national accounting, this implies going beyond the economic theory explanation and taking a broader view of the history of the countries where national accounts have developed over three and a half centuries. As the four unanswered questions discussed above clearly demonstrate, the history of economic thought alone is not sufficient to answer our key question. Economic theory is too general, and isolated historical events are too specific, to serve as consistent explanations for the heterogeneous and non-linear development of national accounting across time and space. We must, at this point, step outside the economist's traditional comfort zone and look at the wider political history, in Europe as well as its offshoots, which helped shape the structure and content of the accounts at different times and places.

Our alternative hypothesis is that estimating national income arose as quantitative political rhetoric. While many authors are aware of the title of Sir William Petty's founding work in this field – *Political Arithmetick* – the common view is that it designates statistics, i.e. data on the state as a polity (as opposed to business data or school arithmetic). We show below that rather than merely serving as data on the state, estimates of national income were conceived and constructed as statistical rhetoric with political goals. To paraphrase Milton Friedman, national accounting is always and everywhere a political phenomenon, in the sense that its chief purpose is to argue in favor of or against particular economic policies, or to demonstrate the (relative) power of various states or classes.

The quote from Marx above becomes relevant at this point. The historical literature on national accounting described above assumes it to be chiefly a statistical exercise, which may be useful for policy makers, but is at its core mostly an objective, data- and theory-driven process. The main thesis of this part of the book, however, is that national accounting across time and place has been more akin to numerical rhetoric – advocating for particular policies – than to statistical fact finding. That is, beyond attempting to describe, interpret, or measure the world, the designers of national accounts (which, until the twentieth century, were one and the same as the compilers of the data) attempted to change the economic world – through arguing for or against particular policies as well as portraying the relative power of nations or classes.

Thus, instead of the cliché of evidence-based policy justifying the use of national accounts data for policy decisions (e.g. austerity measures), what emerges is the opposite (and novel) notion of policy-based evidence. National accounts are complex systems of economic data, socially constructed, and, unlike more straightforward macroeconomic indicators – such as the rate of unemployment – leave plenty of room for maneuver in their design. This flexibility is both the effect and the cause of the accounts being developed and used to advocate for specific policies by the architects of these intricate datasets. The next five sections provide detailed evidence to support this thesis, documenting the evolution of national accounting through five distinct phases: the rise of the nation-state, the Pax Britannica, the advent of central economic planning, the Statistical Cold War, and the rise of finance since 1992.

3.2 The rise of the nation-state – international competition and national economic policies

Focusing on economic power and policies as the explanatory factors in the evolution of national accounts allows us to resolve the four riddles that arise due to the literature's emphasis on economic theory as the key determinant of national accounting structure and content across time and space. Recall that the first puzzle related to the timing and location of the first national accounting estimates, namely seventeenth-century England and France (as well as to the later arrival of this practice in other countries such as Germany, Italy, and the United States).

Richard Stone, one of the key protagonists in the development of national accounts in the twentieth century (both in the UK and globally), also pondered the timing and location of the first national income estimates, in his foreword to Pyatt and Roe's book *Social Accounting for Development Planning with Special Reference to Sri Lanka*: "Why was it that the kind of work done by King, Davenant, Graunt and Petty seems to have died with their generation and to have taken a very long time to pick up?" (Pyatt and Roe, 1977, xvii). He offered the following explanation in his 1984 Nobel Memorial Lecture:

> To trace the origins of national economic accounting we must go back to seventeenth century England, an age of great intellectual vigor, scientific curiosity and inventiveness. William Petty, physician, chemist, land surveyor, cartographer, naval engineer, co-founder of the Royal Society, adviser both to the Cromwell government and after the Restoration to Charles II and, above all, political arithmetician, was one of the more remarkable products of that remarkable century.
>
> (Stone, 1984)

Vanoli also wonders about the reasons for "this English innovation at the end of the 17th century" (Vanoli, 2005, 11), and quotes an explanation offered by Phyllis Deane (1955):

> An important factor in this new combination of circumstances was the spirit of the age. The end of the seventeenth century was a period of eager interest in experimental science of all kinds and in the systematic pursuit of scientific knowledge for its own sake. It was characteristic of the age that writers on political and economic matters should begin to comprehend the economic system as a whole and should try to describe it in quantitative terms.
>
> (Deane, 1955, 3)

The reasons Studenski gives for the occurrence of the first estimates in late seventeenth-century England include this being "one of the most critical periods" in its history, including the civil war and the extreme uncertainty pertaining to it, as well as the threat to England's position as the dominant maritime power "by repeated attacks from Holland and France" (ibid.).

While all of these contextual factors are important, they still do not clearly explain why national income estimating began at this time, and in England and France of all places. After all, civil wars happened before the seventeenth century, and scientific curiosity and experiments were very much in the spirit of the Renaissance. There is no reason, for example, why Leonardo da Vinci could not have dabbled in estimating national income in fifteenth-century Florence. Using our framework, however, we can see that following the Peace of Westphalia in 1648, the sovereign-nation-state was becoming the key political actor in the European scene, overtaking both city-states such as those in Northern Italy and territorial empires such as Spain and the Holy Roman Empire.

National accounts thus appeared at the same time as the rise of nation-states in Europe, first of all in England and France. The Peace of Westphalia, which ended the Thirty Years' War, is widely considered as the beginning of the modern system of nation-states, introducing such principles as the sovereignty of states, their right to self-determination, and their legal equality in international relations. As Giovanni Arrighi points out, "[i]n terms of world power, the principal beneficiaries of the new [Westphalia] system of rule were…France and England. For the next century and a half … the interstate system was dominated by the struggle for world supremacy between these two great powers" (Arrighi, 2010, 48). Not surprisingly, the first occurrences of national income estimates in history are to be found in the second half of the seventeenth century, first in England and shortly after in France. The estimation of national income followed the beginning, a few years earlier, of "the discipline of statistics" with John Graunt's 1662 book on vital statistics, *Natural and Political Observations Made upon the Bills of Mortality* (Studenski, 1958, 26). The early role of demographic statistics for political purposes is evident in the etymology of the word "statistics" itself: (German) *Statistik* – study of political facts and figures; (from New Latin) *statisticus* – of politics, (from Latin) *status* – state (Merriam-Webster Online, *Origin of Statistics*). It was thus no coincidence that such data were first sought and collected by nation-states, for public purposes, exactly at the time when these political entities were developing their consciousness, asserting their power, and exploring various policies.

3.2.1 The purpose of national income estimates

The step from population to economic statistics was short. William Petty (1623–1687), widely considered to be the first to estimate national income, published two such estimates, in 1665 and 1676, the latter in an essay entitled *Political Arithmetick*. Studenski explains the process thus: "By applying the same methods of quantitative observation and analysis to economic phenomena that Graunt had used for population changes, Petty was able to enlarge the scope of this new tool" (ibid.).

The new consciousness and power of the two leading nation-states of the time – England and France – demonstrated itself in the first purposes for which national income estimates were used. William Petty constructed his estimates for two main reasons. One, as Studenski noted, was a comparison of England with France (as well as Holland, a declining though still potent rival). The other purpose highlights the fact that, at this stage in history, economic policies of the nation-state were limited to tariffs and taxation. Petty recommended proportional taxation (10 percent in peacetime and 17.5 percent in wartime), since "universal taxation proportionate to income would be more equitable and less burdensome on the economy than the existing 'irregular taxation' that bore heavily on trade while leaving other segments of the economy almost untouched" (ibid., 29). This is the first documented use of national income estimate to advocate for a specific, concrete economic policy (in this case, fiscal). As we shall see, a tradition was born here that continues to the present day.

Further examples of Petty's policy-driven estimates can be found in the ten principal conclusions he reached, one for each of the chapters in *Political Arithmetick*. The conclusion from Chapter II is that "some kind of Taxes, and Publick Levies, may rather *increase* than diminish the Common-Wealth" (quoted in Studenski, my emphasis). The conclusion from Chapter VIII is "[t]hat there are spare Hands enough among the King of England's Subjects, to earn two Millions per annum, more than they now do, and there are Employments, ready, proper, and sufficient for that purpose" (ibid.). Rather than merely describing the state of the population and income of England, Petty is using his estimates as a call for action – applying progressive taxation and increasing employment, all the while improving the wealth of the nation.

Another example is the work of Sir Matthew Decker (1679–1749), a Member of Parliament from 1719 to 1722, as well as director of the East India Company. "An ardent free trader, he published two essays advocating the repeal of customs duties, proposing that they be replaced by a general tax on houses and buildings (exempting the houses of the poor) and by excises on luxuries. To support his proposal, Decker prepared an estimate of the then current national income (1744)" (ibid., 41). Likewise, Arthur Young's estimates were prepared to advocate a reform of England's tax system consisting of two main changes: introducing a general income tax and abolishing the church tithe.

In 1798, Prime Minister William Pitt made a total income estimate of England, Wales, and Scotland, to support his proposal for Britain's first ever general income tax. It is very telling to note at this point that, intending to exempt all labor income from taxation, Pitt did not estimate labor income at all. This is a clear example of a national income estimate constructed not to describe the general economic picture of a nation but rather delineating its scope, coverage, and content directly based on its advocated policy recommendation.

Pitt's proposed income tax was not without objections, however. Benjamin Bell prepared an estimate of national income in 1799 (with a revision published in 1802) in order to show that "Pitt's proposed income tax would be wholly inadequate to produce the needed increases in the government's revenues as well as effect the desired changes in the distribution of the national tax burden among the different classes of British society" (ibid., 47). Instead he proposed a much more progressive income tax to attain these goals. He also suggested repeal of the Corn Laws, as well as "repeal of all the existing internal excises and customs duties, and replace them with a universal income tax, levied at graduated rates" in order to relieve the tax burden on farmers and shift it to "other, more lightly taxed classes" (ibid., 48). In sum, Bell undertook his estimates with the specific purpose of demonstrating "the inequitableness of the existing tax system, the inadequacies of Pitt's income tax proposal, and the superiority of his own broader tax proposal" (ibid., 48).

National income estimates in France, albeit developing later, were equally if not more motivated by political critiques and agitation for reform. The reasons for the later appearance and slower developments in France compared with England, according to Studenski, included the poorer quality and accessibility of public records, a tax system "incorporating vast exemptions for the rich" as well as "highly arbitrary assessments," and the relative lack of tolerance of the French government of "private inquiries into the country's resources than the more democratic government of England" (ibid., 52). The first two reasons are supported by the fact that "England's tax system was probably more diversified than that of any other country at the time, and was in all likelihood better administered than that of any other country, [which] made the tax records exceptionally useful for calculating the country's national income" (ibid., 33). The third reason is confirmed by the fact that the French nation-state was more absolute and centralized than that of England at this time.

Perhaps not incidentally, French estimators of national income used more incendiary language than their English equivalents. Boisguillebert, a lieutenant-general of Rouen, whom Studenski ruthlessly dubs "one of the world's poorest statisticians even for the time when Political Arithmetic was in its swaddling clothes," nonetheless "made sound and devastating criticisms of the French fiscal system" as a basis for his reform proposals (ibid., 52). In his view, Louis XIV's economic policies were destroying income and wealth in France. Boisguillebert advocated reform, stressing that the true interest of the sovereign "lies in maximizing the incomes and wealth of his people by wise fiscal and other measures" (ibid., 53). Specifically, he advocated the repeal of all taxes except the royal *taille* (but without any exemptions, and in proportion to the property and income of people) and the poll tax, to be imposed uniformly at a low rate on all adults. His claim was that state revenues would increase under this proposal, while encouraging the growth of both agriculture and industry.

Boisguillebert also criticized the mercantilist policies of the French government and advocated a more *laissez-faire* approach. He was an opponent of the prohibition on grain exports instituted by Colbert (Louis XIV's finance minister), reminiscent of England's Corn Laws (the latter were against imports, but had similar effects on trade according to advocates of free trade). Because of government disapproval of his policies, Boisguillebert published his works abroad and anonymously. This was not surprising, given that the title of one of his works can be translated as "France ruined under Louis XIV." He lost his post as lieutenant-general of Rouen and was exiled to the South of France. His compatriot Vauban, who shared his criticism of the regressive tax system of the time, was banished from court for his 1707 book, *Project for a Royal Tithe* (which was promptly suppressed by the government).

By contrast, the French Physiocrats, while theoretically "more advanced [than economists in] England ... in the statistical substance of [their] estimates [were] many years behind" (ibid., 77). This fits well with both the Physiocrats being considered the first school of thought in the history of economic theory and our assertion that the history of economic thought is not a good guide to the history of national accounting.

3.2.2 The institutional context of national income estimates

The scope of economic policy shaping the estimates also determined the institutional setup for their preparation. Before the twentieth century, "[Initiative came from individuals" (Vanoli, 2005, 4). Surveying the 260 years of what he calls "intermittent estimates of national income," Vanoli observes that over this long period, "no state is known to have placed any specific order for this type of product" (ibid., 3). On the face of it, this is an anomaly, given the fact that national accounting and the nation-state appeared roughly at the same time. This does make sense, however, since wider economic policy issues (full employment, price stability, industrial policies, etc.) at this point were not on the agendas of nation-states, which were concerned mostly with tax and tariff matters at the time.

The limited nature of economic policy in this period explains another closely related institutional aspect: the fact that, among those individuals who did take the initiative in the early period of national income estimating, "no professional statisticians can be mentioned until the middle and mostly the end of the nineteenth century" (ibid., 4). Economists (or political economists, as students of the worldly philosophy were known in this period) are also conspicuously missing from the history of national income estimating at this time. Vanoli explains this puzzle by the fact that "recognized economists did not pay much interest to the quantitative estimation of national income" during these two and a half centuries, while some (such as Say and McCulloch) "openly showed their skepticism" (ibid., 11). Table 3.1 shows the documented occupations of some of the earliest authors of national income estimates.

Beyond the fact that none of these men was a statistician or a political economist, the breadth and variety of their occupations attests to the general "social and political concerns of their authors, generally associated with some projects of reform" (ibid., 4).

3.2.3 The rise of national income estimates in Germany and Italy

Now that our theory explains why national accounting first emerged in seventeenth-century England and France, as well as its institutional setup in this early period, it remains for us to investigate the second part of Question 1, namely why the practice appeared almost two centuries later in other countries. Studenski's answer to this riddle is as follows: "Advances in transportation and communication had brought the nations of the western world into closer contact with one another, making it possible for them to exchange their intellectual and scientific heritages" (Studenski, 129). As we shall see below, however, this technological explanation misses the mark since communication and transportation technologies themselves do not explain why national accounting took root at this period only in some countries and not in others, which experienced similar technical advances.

Starting with Germany, Studenski suggests yet another reason for its lateness relative to France and England in the field of national accounting. In the nineteenth century, Germany was advanced in the theory of

Table 3.1 Occupations of national income pioneers

Name	*Country*	*Occupations*
William Petty	England	Professor of Anatomy (at Oxford); physician; Member of Parliament; chief land surveyor and tax administrator of Ireland
Gregory King	England	Herald; cartographer; engraver; surveyor; registrar at the College of the Army; secretary to the Comptrollers Accounts
Charles Davenant	England	Member of Parliament; Commissioner of excise; Inspector general of imports and exports
Pierre le Pesant de Boisguillebert	France	Lieutenant-governor of Rouen
Marshall Vauban	France	Retired army engineer
Henry Beeke	England	Clergyman; Professor of Modern History and Dean (at Bristol)
Benjamin Bell	England	Surgeon; practical and scientific agriculturalist

Source: Based on Vanoli (2005, 4) as well as Studenski (1958, various sections)

national income but not in its measurement, since German economists were mostly skeptical of the accuracy and usability of national income estimates. By 1872, however, seventeen German *Länder* (states) had their own statistical offices which began making such estimates. The two motivations Studenski suggests for this interest include "a vigorous socialist movement" and the "introduction in Prussia and some of the other states of proportional and progressive income taxes" (Studenski, 135). While these two factors may have had some role to play, our hypothesis of national accounting as political rhetoric suggests another, more critical development. German unification in 1871 happened right around the time of the first four estimates of national income: Rümelin's 1863 estimate for Württemberg, and the estimates of Engol (1868), Soetbeer (1873), and Samter (1875) for Prussia. It did take until 1899 for the first estimate of the whole country by R. E. May, and on the eve of World War I, in 1913, Karl Helfferich published the "first truly comprehensive estimate for the whole of Germany", and concluded that "France is considerably behind Germany in national income" (ibid., 144). This is not sufficient evidence to establish causality, of course, but the timing of the beginning of national accounting practice in German states does suggest that political forces – rather than merely theoretical and technical factors – may have also contributed to this development.

The case of Italy is very similar, where "toward the end of the [nineteenth] century, theoretical economics again flourished, [but] statistics were backward" (Studenski, 137). Matteo Pantaleoni published an estimate of the wealth and its distribution in Italy in the 1880s. And while Studenski notes in passing that it was "following the unification of Italy," he does not seem to consider it more than a coincidence (the process of Risorgimento (unification) in Italy began in 1815 with the Congress of Vienna, and ended in 1870). Our theory, however, suggests that rising national awareness may have propelled national income estimates in Italy, as it did in Germany, France, and England before it.

3.3 Pax Britannica – the unique phase of British hegemony

The second of the four questions mentioned above relates to the paucity of estimates in England and France between the late seventeenth century and the early twentieth century. Indeed, aside from the appearance of national income estimates in Italy and Germany around the time of their unification, the nineteenth century is the sparsest period in the history of national accounting (Studenski, 124). This seems especially bizarre given that this was the most glorious period in the history of economic thought, encompassing the work of Adam Smith, David Ricardo, John Stuart Mill, and Karl Marx, to name just the most famous.

Our political-history framework, however, sheds light on this hiatus of national accounting. Modelski (1978) considers nineteenth-century Britain a unique example of "a historical world power ... monopolizing (i.e., controlling more than half of) the market for (or the supply of) order-keeping in the global layer of interdependence" (216). This situation changed the balance of power in Europe, leading to a relatively stable century of Pax Britannica. As Hobsbawm observes, "there was no war involving more than two great powers between 1815 and 1914" (1996, 99). The main developments in national accounting during this time, therefore, all took place in countries engaging in combined development to contest British industrial and imperial supremacy (Desai, 2013, 43).

Russian national income estimates emerged in 1896 when V. I. Pokrovsky's work was published. This late appearance is given two explanations by Studenski: "political conditions were not favorable to any statistical and economic research having political implications" (137–138), and, as in Germany, there was a lack of interest in the topic of national income. However, Pokrovsky focused on Russia's turn from a free trade policy to economic protectionism and the resulting tariff war with Germany between 1892 and 1894, and wished to "appraise the merits of this new policy." In 1906, Propokovitch's estimated national income and found that Russians were poorer even than Bulgarians and Serbs.

The cases of Europe's offshoots are more complicated because their histories were connected to, and their institutions imported from, their mother countries (for instance, from England in the case of the United States and Australia). Nevertheless, their industrialization occurred more contemporaneously to their mother countries, and our explanatory variables also work for the timing and motivation for the beginning of national income estimates in these countries.

Australia has the honor of being the first country in which an official government estimate of national income was undertaken, in 1886–1887, by Timothy A. Coghlan, a government statistician, for the province of New South Wales. While there had been British colonies in the continent since 1788, the modern nation-state of Australia was created only in a 1901 referendum in which the colonies of the time decided to become a federation. It is thus timely that Coghlan extended his early estimates to "an annual series covering all the seven colonies of Australasia" starting in 1890 (Studenski, 135). These estimates were also the first "modern estimates to embrace all three aspects of national income – its production, distribution, and disposition – and to employ the three estimating methods associated with national income's three phases" (ibid.).

In the United States, the second industrial revolution culminated in the Gilded Age of huge fortunes and historically unprecedented inequalities. The rise of the Populist Party, the depression of 1893, and the Pullman strike in 1894 (organized by the American Railway Union against the Pullman company and the main railroads and put down by federal troops) formed the background of increased class consciousness and tension against which national accounting in the United States began in earnest in 1896. Here, unlike Australia, it was the rise of economic policy issues and class tensions to the national level (rather than the unification of the country) that appears to have given an impetus to the development of national accounting, though class tensions were heightened by the closure of the frontier as the US's "continental expansion came up against rival empires, emerging nation-states and the Pacific" (Desai, 2013, 64), ending the period where land was not scarce and labor therefore better compensated than in Western Europe.

While the very first national income estimate in the United States was made by George Tucker (a professor at the University of Virginia) in 1843 (who was interested in finding out the size and structure of US national income), it was limited to a net-value estimate of material production alone. A more thorough and comprehensive estimate appeared only in 1896, in Dr. Charles B. Spahr's book on the distribution of wealth in the United States. The data was presented by distribution of labor and capital income by family-income groups. Spahr's book criticized policies leading to higher concentration of income at that time (federal taxes as well as tariff, railroad, and currency policies), while supporting more regulation of monopolies (especially the railroads), and making taxes on income and property progressive.

In 1915, W. I. King extended Spahr's work in an estimate of the distribution of income and wealth in the United States but derived opposing conclusions which owed more to "his conservative philosophy than … the figures themselves" (Studenski, 143). King opposed social reforms such as that of the "living wage" as "a drift toward socialism" (ibid.). Instead, his recommended policies to achieve prosperity were a combination of birth control and immigration reform.

At this point, Studenski makes a strong and, as we will see below, false claim: "King's was one of the last national income estimates in any country to combine the estimating task with economic politics. Nearly all subsequent national income estimators limited themselves to the preparation of estimates, leaving the task of social, economic and political interpretation of their figures to other individuals" (ibid., 143–144). This statement mistakes a change in the institutional unit undertaking the estimates – from individual persons to government statistical offices – for a change in the purpose of national accounting. Political concerns persisted as both motivations and determinants of national accounting, though they became less transparent and more difficult to discern. Documenting the continuing role of power as a driver of measurement is our task in the next three sections.

3.4 The return of international competition and the advent of central economic planning

The third question left unanswered by technocratic histories of national accounting is why the early decades of the twentieth century saw a revival in national accounting after a relative stagnation. Common wisdom credits Keynesian theory and improvements in econometric methods (Bos, Studenski, Tily, and Vanoli). As we saw above, however, government estimates of national accounting began to appear in force over a decade before the publication of the *General Theory* in 1936 (Canada and the USSR in 1925, Germany in 1929, the Netherlands and New Zealand in 1931, the United States in 1934, and Turkey in 1935). Instead, two geopolitical developments account for this revival. First, as Modelski (1978) writes, "[b]y 1900 it had become clear to many that Pax

Britannica was well past its prime and that the world system was swiftly losing its ordering capacities" (223). Inter-state competition was back and stronger than ever after World War I, which signaled "the death of 'liberal capitalism,' the gold standard, and British financial and commercial supremacy" (Desai, 2013, 53). The other new development was a change in how the governments of nation-states perceived themselves. The exigencies of both world wars as well as the global depression saw a shift in state economic roles, from a limited focus on tax and tariff policies to becoming full-fledged economic actors. Furthermore, the decline of empires coupled with decolonization meant that policies to stimulate domestic aggregate demand in the industrialized countries were becoming more important, as witnessed in the "one-off increase in the share of wages in the national income in the postwar period" in both Britain and the United States (Desai, 2015, 206).

Central economic planning was on the rise, and not just in the newly created Soviet Union. This caused a shift in the institutional character of national income estimates, away from individual researchers and toward official government design and compilation of the data. Key issues in this period of national income estimates included the ability of states to mobilize their industrial and human resources to the fullest extent possible (for both war-mongering and reconstruction purposes), to ensure price and wage stability, and in general to coordinate the ever more complex and more national economies of industrialized nations facing wars, economic crises, and social strife.

It was these two geopolitical changes – rather than economic theory – that led, in turn, to two key innovations in national income accounting in this period. First, the input–output analysis developed by Wassily Leontief is today often considered to be a precursor of general equilibrium theory, but it arose in fact out of the socialist calculation debate of the 1920s, as well as from the need for economic planning during World War II. The following quote from Leontief's interview with Duncan Foley is illuminating:

> When the war began, interest in input–output analysis grew. I was kind of a consultant on economic planning. It was for the Air Force, which of course was very important during the war. The best input–output matrix was computed by the Air Force. They had also an input–output table of the German economy, because it enabled them to choose targets. Usually I'm not very pragmatic, but if you want to do something, you have to understand what you're doing, and for the Air Force that was the committed choice of targets and so on, so input–output analysis was very interesting to them.
>
> (Foley, 1998, 17–18)

John Maynard Keynes made another, often misunderstood, contribution to national accounting. Tily (2009), for example, argued that the Keynesian multiplier, developed in the *General Theory*, was key in the rise of modern national accounting. However, the *General Theory* did not contain a full estimate of national income (merely a few figures on the decrease in investment during the Great Depression). It is in Keynes's policy book, *How to Pay for the War* (1940), that we find the now familiar breakdown of GDP by the expenditure approach (i.e. a sum of consumption, investment, government spending, and net exports). Following in the footsteps of 250 years of national income practitioners, Keynes estimated the national income of Great Britain with the explicit purpose of convincing the government and citizenry of the need for deferred civilian consumption. Keynes explicitly presents his policy motivation at the opening of the third chapter:

> In order to calculate the size of the cake which will be left for civilian consumption, we have to estimate (1) the maximum current output that we are capable of organizing from our resources of men and plant and materials, (2) how fast we can safely draw on our foreign reserves by importing more than we export, [and] (3) how much of all this will be used up by our war effort.
>
> (Keynes, 1940)

At this stage, different countries still designed and compiled national income and product statistics in different ways, depending on their needs, data availability, and policy goals. The differences included approach (income, net output, or expenditure), level of detail, and overall structure. Part II of Studenski's book provides examples of national income estimates in the interwar period from Brazil, Canada, France, Germany, Ireland, the Netherlands, New Zealand, Soviet Russia, Sweden, Switzerland, Turkey, the United States, and Yugoslavia. A key feature of the estimates in this period of "extraordinary flourishing," as Studenski calls it, is the inclusion of the government sector – both its wartime and peaceful expenditures – as a consistent part of the estimates. This reflects the "colossal problems of economic reconstruction … colossal shifts that have taken place in the relative economic power of the different nations as a result of the [First World] war … and the need for mobilization of economic resource to meet the threats of another world war" as well as to confront the Great Depression (Studenski, 149). Further causes of this newly found importance of government in the economy were the increased nationalization of economies due to increased international competition and higher rates of labor unionization.

In addition to the earlier income approach used since the first estimate by William Petty in the seventeenth century, more and more countries began using the net output (value added) and expenditure approaches, as these allowed a presentation of the economy by industry as well as by spending category (i.e. consumption, investment, government, and exports/imports). This shift from income-only estimates to estimates including also output and expenditure statistics reflects the more active role of the governments of nation-states. Not only were governments now designing the estimates and collecting the data (both done previously by individual researchers), they were also focusing the content of the estimates on the industrial structure of the economy as well as on their own spending activities with a view to policy making.

3.5 Spurious universalism – the Statistical Cold War

In contrast to the diversity of national income and product estimates up to the end of the World War II, the postwar situation appears on the surface to converge toward a standardization and universalization of estimates. A committee of the League of Nations met in Bretton Woods, New Hampshire, in 1944 to agree on national income concepts and structures, "to make them more comparable and useful" (Studenski, 154). This work was later taken on by the United Nations and culminated in the *System of National Accounts* in 1953. It was the first international standard to govern the design and structure of national accounts, although the compilation of data and actual estimation remained the work of individual governments. Had national accounting ceased to be a national political tool reflecting countries' position in international rivalries as well as advocating for national economic policies? This is certainly the view in the technocratic histories of national accounting mentioned above.

In reality, however, the interstate rivalry had not disappeared, merely shifted from the level of the individual nation-state to that of bloc rivalry during the Cold War. As Desai explains, in the postwar period the very existence of the USSR "ensured … that combined development … had to be tolerated in recovering economies" (Desai, 2013, 53). The emergence of non-capitalist combined development had its statistical equivalent: the USSR created its own standard of national accounting – the *Material Product System* (MPS), and SNA 1968 was influenced by and partly harmonized with the MPS (United Nations, 1968, 1), particularly by disaggregating the production account of SNA 1953 into input–output accounts. This allowed comparison between the two systems, thus acknowledging the bipolar and contested nature of national accounting at this time, rather than supporting the universalization or hegemony view enshrined by Studenski and others, for instance when Studenski proclaimed that "in the twentieth century, the preparation and publication of annual national income estimates has become universal" (Studenski, 142).

The MPS, also known as the System of Material Balances, is another proof that politics rather than theory shaped national accounting. As Studenski points out early in his book, the system championed by the USSR was not based on Marx's theory of productive versus non-productive activities but rather on Adam Smith's narrow production concept. The latter considered only industries producing material goods to be productive, relegating all services to a non-productive status and excluding them from the accounts. The irony of an avowedly Marxist regime adopting a concept of productiveness from Adam Smith, of all political economists, supports our thesis that theory regularly took a back seat to political motives in the history of national accounting.

3.6 Spurious globalization and the financialization of national accounting

The final unsolved question relates to the revision of the SNA in 1993. At a theoretical level, economics has been undergoing an anti-Keynesian revolution since the 1970s, with New Classical economics and monetarism leading the way. Why, then, did the changes in national accounting lag economic theory by a generation? The previous section demonstrated how the Cold War contributed to the development of a bipolar system of national accounting. A major change in this situation had to await the end of the Cold War and the fall of the Berlin Wall in 1989.

The geopolitical economy of the international standard-making of national accounts began to gradually change in the lead-up to the end of the Cold War. While the first two SNAs in 1953 and 1968 were strictly standards created under the aegis of the United Nations, in the early 1980s the responsibility of reviewing, updating, and publishing the SNA moved to a new body, the Intersecretariat Working Group on National Accounts (ISWGNA). This is "one of the oldest interagency bodies set up by the United Nations Statistical Commission (UNSC) to enhance cooperation among international organizations working in the same field" (United Nations, ISWGNA). Besides the UN, the ISWGNA includes the EU, the Organisation for Economic Co-operation and Development (OECD), the IMF, and the World Bank. The latter two are international financial institutions, while the former two are clubs of mostly wealthy countries. This change in membership is indicative of the shift in the balance of power from a truly universal organization – the UN – to institutions dominated by developed and financialized countries. It also reflects the departure from the view that statistics are the responsibility of governments to one assigning a greater role to financial institutions (whether international or national) in revising such standards. The prominence of banks in the review process leading to SNA 2008, for example, was significant: organizations as well as countries were permitted to comment on the forty-four issues selected for discussion. Of the seventy-four comments listed on the United Nations Statistics Division's (UNSD) website, thirty-four were from national (central) or regional banks, whereas the remaining forty were from national statistical offices. Similarly, during the revision process of SNA 1993, "the internationalist aspirations of the 1993 SNA received a further boost from the fall of the Berlin Wall" (OECD, 2014). The former Soviet republics abandoned the MPS they had used until the early 1990s, and adopted the SNA (along with China, Mongolia, and Vietnam). Rather than globalization, however, this constituted a shift from Cold War competition of East and West to a post-Cold War competition of the developed (and increasingly financialized) North and the developing South.

The 1993 revision of the SNA was the first to explicitly recognize financial intermediation as productive, using the concept of financial intermediation services indirectly measured (FISIM) to impute value added to these activities. Of the three revisions made to this international standard since the original 1953 SNA, this took the longest – twenty-five years since the previous revision, in 1968. Besides the novel concept of FISIM, SNA 1993 contained "clarifications and justifications of the concepts presented … harmonized with other related statistical systems Gross Domestic Power and … introduce[d] a number of features that reflect[ed] new analytical and policy concerns of countries and international organizations" (United Nations, 1993, 648). One such new feature to note was the harmonization of the SNA with the fifth edition of the IMF's *Balance of Payments Manual* (*BPM5*).

Coming to the specific definition of financial services in SNA 1993, these included financial intermediation, which involves "financial risk management and liquidity transformation, activities in which an institutional unit incurs financial liabilities for the purpose of acquiring mainly financial assets" (United Nations, 2009, 114). SNA 2008 further enlarged the definition of financial services as compared with SNA 1993:

> The 2008 SNA defines financial services more explicitly than in the 1993 SNA … to ensure that the increases in financial services other

> than the financial intermediation, specifically risk management and liquidity transformation, are captured. Financial services include monitoring services, convenience services, liquidity provision, risk assumption, underwriting and trading services.
>
> (United Nations, 2009, 581)

SNA 2008 thus does not stop at the traditional justification for the productivity of financial institutions, i.e. intermediation between depositors and lenders. The biggest change, however, was that for financial intermediaries, all loans and deposits were included, not just those made from intermediated funds (United Nations, 2009, 583).

The meaning of this change cannot be overstated. Whereas with financial intermediation a semblance of providing a (productive) service was maintained, this new inclusion of banks' own funds in the production boundary basically meant that any act of speculation, using one's own funds invested for profit, was now deemed productive by definition.

As mentioned above, the proposed "adaptation" to the production boundary included two major new ideas:

- including activities other than intermediation as output of financial firms;
- inclusion of banks' own funds in the calculation of FISIM.

As discussed above, the history of the first three SNAs in terms of treatment of financial services revolved around the concept of intermediation. SNA 1953 treated it as not productive, SNA 1968 as only implicitly productive, while SNA 1993, for the first time, defined it as two separately productive activities – borrowing and lending. The ideas that financial services are productive beyond intermediation, and that within intermediation the use of banks' own funds can be counted as productive, are thus both far more radical than SNA 2008 presents them to be. However, the official view is that SNA 2008 was not a major departure from SNA 1993, as stated in the Preface to the new SNA: "The changes between the 1993 SNA and the 2008 SNA are … less extensive than the changes introduced in 1993."

The 2008 revision process was not without objections. The German statistical office, for example, questioned "whether the absolute difference between the reference rate and the actual interest rates can be interpreted in total as remuneration for a service. In our view, there is a remuneration for risk assumption included, which *does not represent a productive activity* as no input of labor and/or capital is needed" (United Nations, Global Review, emphasis added). Statistics Netherlands, on the other hand, held the opposite view: "in relation to a recent discussion on the exclusion of the risk element from the implicit service charge, we still have to be convinced about the need to exclude such a risk element" (ibid.). Perhaps most telling is the comment by the European Central Bank (ECB) on recording flows in financial instruments, especially deposits and loans:

> No exclusion is made for lending of own funds. Although the act of lending and the charging of SNA interest is *not a productive activity*, there is a service charge associated with lending. A person borrowing from a bank is unaware of whether the amounts borrowed are of intermediated funds or come from the bank's own funds and no difference in the service charges applied should be made.
>
> (Ibid., my emphasis)

This view clearly exemplifies a break from the industrial and productive focus and a turn to a neoclassical placement of subjective utility at the center of economic activity (i.e. whatever people are willing to pay for on the market is deemed productive by definition). This change had the effect of breaching the production boundary and essentially allowing anything to be counted in GDP.

4 The financialization of GDP

> Use-value, not exchange-value, is the purpose of the whole system of production.
>
> (Karl Marx, 1867, 50)

> All production is for the purpose of ultimately satisfying a consumer.
>
> (John Maynard Keynes, 1936, 46)

4.1 Accounting for finance

The three major types of financial services are treated in the national accounts in three different ways. Capital gains are excluded a priori from the production accounts, interest flows generated by financial intermediation are treated as an intermediate input to other industries and deducted from GDP, and fee-based financial services are considered productive and are imputed a value added based on net revenue. While there is consensus regarding the exclusion of capital gains since there is no productive activity associated with them, the other two treatments – of interest-based financial intermediation and fee-based financial services – are more controversial. Furthermore, there is an inconsistency in how the standard accounting framework treats these two sources of financial income.

After reviewing some of the technical issues involved in the debate over the assumed productiveness (or lack thereof) of interest-yielding financial intermediation services, we highlight the fact that far less attention has been paid to fee-based financial revenues. Unlike the interest-based part of financial incomes, the fees generated from financial services are not netted out of GDP and thus show up as value added on the production (output) side of the accounts. We assess the differences between finance and the other sectors for which value added is imputed, both conceptually and empirically, and show that it is always an input (or a cost) for other industries and the economy as a whole. We then construct an alternative measure of overall economic activity which treats finance as a cost to be deducted from total value added, consistent with the way FISIM income is treated in the standard accounts.

GDP "is the primary indicator of economic activity and … can be estimated in three ways, which are theoretically equal" (Lee, 2012), although due to differences in sources and methods used in the three approaches, the results can differ and must be reconciled by various processes.

The expenditure approach to GDP is the sum of all final expenditures and is denoted by the familiar equation GDP = C + I + G + X − M (that is, the sum of consumption or final expenditure by households, investment by firms, government final consumption, and net exports). The income approach, by contrast, adds up wages, profits, interest, and taxes minus subsidies. Finally, the production (output) approach to GDP sums up all activities deemed productive[1] across industries:

$$\text{GDP} = \Sigma(Y_i - IC_i) + \text{taxes on products} - \text{subsidies on products} \quad (1)$$

where Y stands for output, IC stands for intermediate consumption, and the terms in the summation expression represent value added for each industry i.

GDP is thus equal to value added plus taxes minus subsidies. As Lee explains, "[o]utput is all the goods and services produced, whilst intermediate consumption comprises all the goods and services consumed or transformed in a production process. The taxes and subsidies are included in order to put all three approaches on a consistent valuation basis" (ibid.). In other words, value added itself is not directly comparable to GDP by the expenditure or income approaches, and we must use GDP by the output approach (i.e. value added + taxes − subsidies) to make comparisons with the other two GDP measures more accurate.

Next, when discussing value added in "finance," the official System of National Accounts includes financial intermediation, insurance and pension funds, and other activities such as administration of financial markets. Some authors (such as Basu and Foley) add real estate, resulting in the FIRE acronym. It is important to note, however, that even the narrow definition of finance which refers only to financial services (and does not include real estate, insurance, or other business services) itself comprises three types of activities performed by the financial industry (including non-bank financial institutions):

1. Services for which banks explicitly charge a fee, and are thus relatively straightforward to record in the national accounts. These

services include overdraft fees, foreign exchange commissions, consulting on mergers and acquisitions, underwriting securities, as well as market-making activities (Akritidis, 2007, Haldane, 2010).

2. Net interest – this part of banks' business is not as easily captured. "Finance – and commercial banking in particular – relies heavily on interest flows as a means of payment for the services they provide. Banks charge an interest rate margin to capture these intermediation services" (Haldane, 2010, 91), which gives rise to the FISIM issue mentioned above.
3. Net spread earnings (NSE), e.g. capital gains or dealing profits from spot trading in the foreign exchange market.

The last item, NSE, is also known as capital gains (or losses), and is already excluded from GDP as a "basic principle of national income accounting" (Oulton, 2013, 7), so we can safely ignore this source of financial income in this discussion.

Thus we are left with the first two types of banking income – income from fee-based financial services and net interest income from financial intermediation. Since fees paid for financial services are easily captured by national accountants, most of the debate has recently focused on the (non-fee-based) net interest part – financial intermediation and the imputation of its output through FISIM. Financial intermediation has long been problematic to measure. Christophers (2011) describes the history of the so-called "banking problem" – the fact that, without imputations, the value added of the financial sector (that is, output minus intermediate consumption) would be negligible or even negative (since if costs are deducted from fee-based revenues alone, the former would often exceed the latter). A useful example is the gross value added (GVA) of the UK financial sector in 2003, which would be £39.8 billion under SNA 1968 (4.1 percent of total GVA). The imputed bank service charge (IBSC), however, was a negative £45.9 billion. Under SNA 1953 the financial sector thus would have shown a negative £6.1 billion value added. "Adopting SNA 1968 had, in effect, *made* UK finance productive" (Christophers, 2011, 130, emphasis in original). Table 4.1 illustrates this point.

At a first stage in the history of this question (SNA 53 and before), all financial intermediation activities were excluded from calculations of national output based on the value-added approach, since they were considered to be mere transfers of funds (similar to social security payments) and hence unproductive. An intermediate approach followed with the United Nations 1968 System of National Accounts (SNA 68), where the output of the financial sector was considered to be an input

Table 4.1 The banking problem with UK data for 2003 using SNA 53 vs. SNA 68

Item	*Amount*		*% of total value added*	
	SNA 1953	*SNA 1968*	*SNA 1953*	*SNA 1968*
Gross value added (GVA) for total economy	£970,700,000,000	£970,700,000,000	100.0%	100.0%
Financial intermediation GVA	£39,800,000,000	£39,800,000,000	4.1%	4.1%
Imputed bank service charge (IBSC)	£45,900,000,000	£45,900,000,000	4.7%	4.7%
GVA for dummy sector	None	−£45,900,000,000	None	−4.7%
Financial intermediation GVA (after IBSC)	−£6,100,000,000	£39,800,000,000	−0.6%	4.1%

Source: United Nations Statistics Division, UN data portal

to a notional (i.e. imaginary) industry which has no output. In spite of the bizarre nature of this approach, "ascribing a negative income to an imaginary industry sector ... has probably been the most used for financial intermediation services in the entire history of Western national accounting" (Christophers, 2011, 130). Finally, with the 1993 SNA, financial intermediation became an explicitly productive activity, for which value added is imputed based on the net interest received by financial institutions (the FISIM approach). The latest revision, SNA 2008, extends the boundaries of SNA 1993 to include ever more exotic financial "products."

As can be seen from Table 4.2,[2] the FIRE sector is bigger under SNA 68 (in absolute terms) since it includes FISIM (line 14), which is then deducted from value added to derive GDP (thus affecting only the relative size of the financial sector rather than the total GDP). In SNA 93, however, FISIM is not deducted as it is already distributed to various uses (i.e. industries purchasing financial intermediation services). As a consequence, several industries show a lower value added (in absolute terms) under SNA 93 than when one uses the SNA 68 approach (agriculture, hunting, forestry and fishing; mining and quarrying; manufacturing; electricity, gas, and water supply; public administration and defense; compulsory social security).

Table 4.2 GDP for the United States, data for 1996, according to SNA 68 vs. SNA 93

Line	*SNA 68*		*SNA 93*	
	Millions of current US$	*% of total value added*	*Millions of current US$*	*% of total value added*
(1) Agriculture, hunting, forestry; fishing	132,500,000,000	1.7%	130,400,000,000	1.8%
(2) Mining and quarrying	115,500,000,000	1.5%	113,000,000,000	1.6%
(3) Manufacturing	1,343,500,000,000	17.5%	1,316,000,000,000	18.3%
(4) Electricity, gas, and water supply	211,000,000,000	2.7%	208,300,000,000	2.9%
(5) Construction	310,100,000,000	4.0%	316,400,000,000	4.4%
(6) Wholesale, retail trade, repair of motor vehicles, motorcycles, and personal and households goods; hotels and restaurants	1,239,800,000,000	16.1%	1,373,300,000,000	19.1%
(7) Transport, storage, and communications	438,800,000,000	5.7%	513,000,000,000	7.2%
(8) Financial intermediation; real estate, renting, and business activities	2,111,500,000,000	27.4%	2,086,000,000,000	29.1%
(9) Public administration and defense; compulsory social security	839,000,000,000	10.9%	591,600,000,000	8.2%
(10) Education; health and social work; other community, social, and personal services	847,300,000,000	11.0%	1,058,300,000,000	14.8%
(11) Private households with employed persons		0.0%	12,000,000,000	0.2%
(12) Plus: statistical discrepancy	107,300,000,000	1.4%		0.0%
(13) Equals: VALUE ADDED, GROSS, in basic prices	7,695,300,000,000	100.0%	7,172,000,000,000	100.0%
(14) Less: financial intermediation services indirectly measured (FISIM)	263,700,000,000	3.4%		0.0%
(15) Plus: taxes less subsidies on products	19,200,000,000	0.2%	546,200,000,000	7.6%
(16) Plus: statistical discrepancy	(32,200,000,000)	−0.4%	32,800,000,000	0.5%
(17) Equals: GROSS DOMESTIC PRODUCT	7,418,600,000,000	96.4%	7,751,100,000,000	108.1%

Even within the 1993 FISIM framework, however, there are two possible estimation methodologies. The approach recommended by SNA 93 is to allocate FISIM across the sectors and industries that use these services, in order to "identify the purchase of these services explicitly and to classify them as intermediate consumption, final consumption expenditure or exports according to which sector incurs the expenditure" (Akritidis, 2007, 30). Use of this approach gives rise to Oulton's argument that "if banking output has been overstated, then the output of some other industry or industries must have been understated" (Oulton, 2013, 3). However, given practical difficulties with allocating FISIM to users (because of conceptual and data availability problems), SNA 93 allows for a simpler approach, which treats all of FISIM as the intermediate consumption of a "nominal sector" (similar to the SNA 68 method). Using this more simplified approach, "GDP is not affected by the size of the FISIM output" (ibid.). Oulton further argues that even using the first approach, the FISIM component has a negligible effect on GDP growth estimation (Oulton, 2013, 6). This observation notwithstanding, the FISIM approach still distorts the relative size of the financial and other sectors within the economy.

Two comments are appropriate at this stage. First, different countries use different approaches based on their preferences, data availability, and conceptual choices. The United Kingdom and several other European countries use the "nominal" sector approach, while the United States (since 1996) distributes FISIM to uses, as shown in Table 4.2. Second, the relative shares of FISIM vs. fee-based services in overall financial incomes have changed over time. As Akritidis observes, the share of FISIM income in total banking income declined from 72 percent in 1992 to 66 percent in 2004), while "the share taken by explicit charges, such as fees and commissions, rose" (Akritidis, 2007, 30).

This fact, as well as the existence of a simpler FISIM approach which does not affect overall GDP, raises the following question: why are fee-based financial services treated as value added, while interest-based financial intermediation is netted out of GDP as intermediate consumption (of either a nominal sector or the total economy)? This inconsistency is understandable from a measurement point of view, since fee-based financial services are easy to capture and therefore present less of an empirical problem than the FISIM issue. From a theoretical point of view, however, the non-FISIM part of financial services, that is, the fee-based income in the GDP-by-output approach, is as problematic. Finance, in its various manifestations, ultimately involves the transfer of money. Unlike other commodities, money has no use intrinsic value, only an exchange value. In fact, it is exchange value par excellence. Gold and silver still had some practical uses when they were the common means of payment, but fiat money is merely symbolic purchasing power. As the textbooks tell us, money serves as a unit of account, means of exchange, and store of value. Neither consumers nor firms can directly consume money, but rather purchase goods and services with it, either for final consumption or as intermediate consumption in the production process.[3]

From a Keynesian point of view, this may seem problematic as money provides people (both consumers and investors) with a liquidity premium, allowing them to hedge against an uncertain future. This notion, however, runs into two problems, one conceptual and one empirical. First, money may indeed confer a feeling of security (or "psychic income") on its holder because of uncertainty, but its contribution to the holder's well-being emanates from its ability to be spent, at a future moment, on goods and services. Money itself cannot be directly consumed but performs the function of store of value in the face of uncertainty. Second, from a practical point of view, even if we accept that money has use-value based on the liquidity premium idea, measuring it would be hard given that its opportunity cost – interest income – is not fixed. Aside from the existence of multiple interest rates for various assets, even changes in the headline or reference interest rate would change the value of money as measured by the liquidity premium. This gives rise to the FISIM problem mentioned above.

Furthermore, fiat money is not really "produced" in the way other goods and services are. In a fractional reserve system, commercial banks lend out more than the high-powered money they have on reserve with the central bank, thus "creating" money. They make their profits by lending out money at a higher interest rate than that which they pay on deposits taken in, and doing other, more complicated things, all of which, however, are ultimately connected to the provision of money. In addition to this, reinforcing money's lack of use-value, it suggests that finance may not have the same relationship between output and employment as other sectors with more directly usable output do. Thus we need to empirically examine whether finance is indeed exceptional in this sense vis-à-vis others sectors of the economy.

4.2 Financial services versus other service sectors for which value added is imputed

As the discussion above suggests, our focus here is on the treatment of finance in national accounting, rather than on imputation issues per se. Finance is conceptually different than other service sectors for which value added is also imputed as explained above. This is also borne out by looking at sectoral shares of total value added and employment. Data from the OECD Structural Analysis (STAN) database is available for these two variables, by industry. Figure 4.1 shows the various relationships between shares in total value added and shares in total employment for the United States.

As the charts in Figure 4.1 show, all sectors except finance and real estate have a close correlation between their shares of total value added and their shares of total employment. Only the latter two sectors display a serious disconnect, with a flat employment share but fluctuations in (imputed) value added. Table 4.3 further shows the correlation coefficients for each industry.

The industries in this table can be grouped in three categories:

- High correlation and statistically significant:
  - agriculture
  - electricity, gas, and water supply
  - construction
  - manufacturing
  - community, social, and personal services.
- Low correlation and statistically significant:
  - transportation, storage, and communications
  - mining and quarrying.
- Low or negative correlation and NOT statistically significant:
  - wholesale and retail trade
  - real estate activities.
- Negative correlation AND statistically significant:
  - financial intermediation.

Thus, for example, while value added is also imputed for community, social, and personal services, the relationship between the values imputed based on incomes, on the one hand, and employment generated in these industries, on the other hand, is positive and statistically significant. By contrast, value added shares in the two FIRE sectors – finance and real estate – seem to be oscillating with negative correlation to employment shares in these industries. Looking at the last column of Table 4.3, finance seems to have a statistically significant (negative) correlation, whereas the correlation of value added and employment shares in real estate is not statistically significant, implying that there is simply no relationship between value added and employment in this sector.

These results could be interpreted in several ways. One interpretation would see finance as destroying rather than creating jobs. Another, more

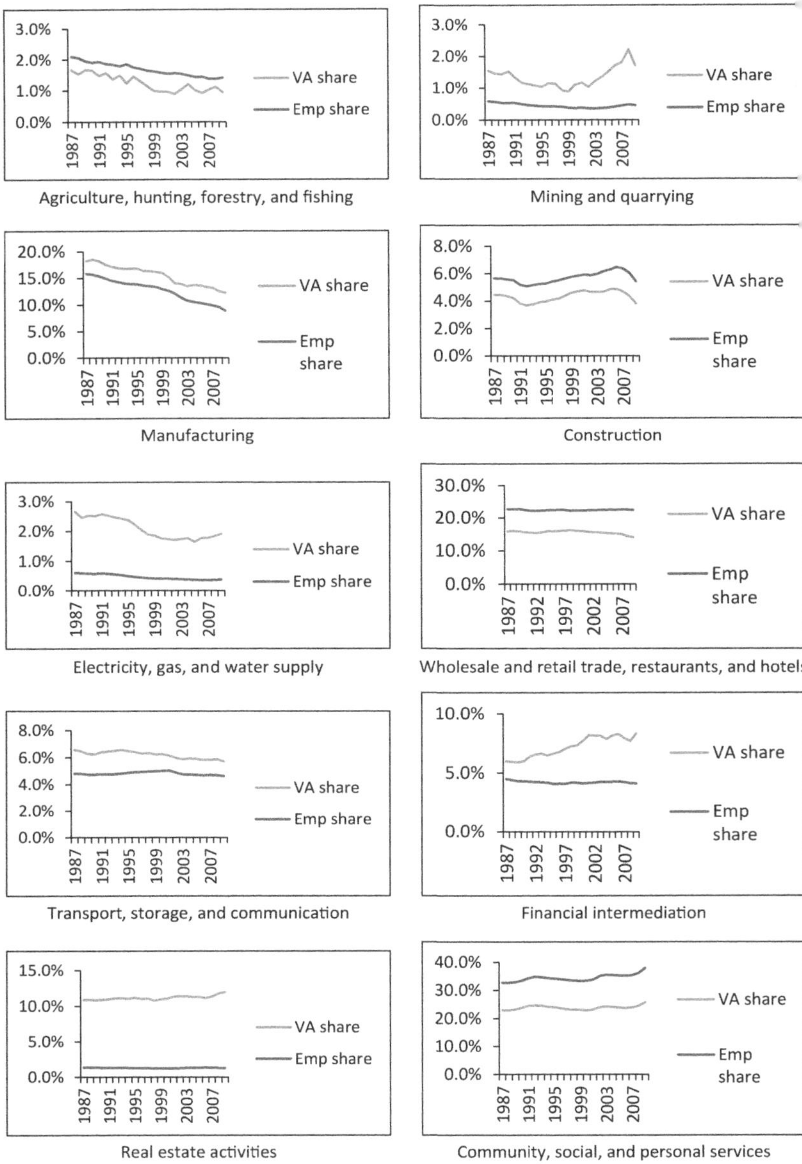

Figure 4.1 Percentage shares of total value added and total employment for various industries in the United States, 1987–2009

Table 4.3 Coefficients of correlation between shares of value added and shares of employment, by industry, US, 1987–2009

Industry	*Correlation between value added and employment shares*	*p-value*
Agriculture, forestry, fishing, and hunting	0.87	0.00
Mining and quarrying	0.39	0.07
Electricity, gas, and water supply	0.97	0.00
Construction	0.91	0.00
Manufacturing	0.99	0.00
Wholesale and retail trade	−0.16	0.46
Transportation, storage, and communications	0.44	0.03
Financial intermediation	−0.42	0.05
Real estate activities	−0.15	0.50
Community, social, and personal services	0.85	0.00

Source: OECD STAN database

naïve version would consider this anomaly to be evidence of outstanding productivity increases in the financial sector, enabling it to produce far more output with less labor input.[4] However, the negative correlation could also signal a problem with the specific measurement of output for this industry. This fits with the idea that increasing the creation of use-value is related to an increase in employment, while increasing the transfer of exchange value (money) is not.

Looking at the matter more formally, we can use the following definitions:

- Sector i's share of employment is $\sigma_i^e = \frac{N_i}{N}$, where N_i is employment in sector i and N is total employment in the economy.
- Sector i's share of output is $\sigma_i^y = \frac{Y_i}{Y}$, where Y_i is output in sector i and Y is total output in the economy.
- Sector i's productivity is $P_i = \frac{Y_i}{N_i}$
- Average productivity in the economy is $P = \frac{Y}{N}$

If all sectors of the economy are productive, the relationship between sectoral employment shares and output shares would be mediated by each sector's labor productivity relative to the average productivity:

$$\sigma_i^e \frac{P_i}{P} = \sigma_i^y \tag{2}$$

where σ_i^e is sector i's share of employment, p_i is sector i's productivity, p is average productivity, and σ_i^y is sector i's share of output. This can be rearranged as follows:

$$\sigma_i^e = \sigma_i^y \frac{P}{P_i} \tag{3}$$

In other words, we expect a sector's share of total employment to be related to its share of output through its productivity relative to the average productivity in the economy. As the latter can never be negative (i.e. $p_i/p>>0$), there is indeed a problem with imputing supercharged productivity to the financial sector given the observed negative correlation between its share of value added and its share of employment between 1996 and 2011. Unless one accepts the naïve productivity theory mentioned above (i.e. that the negative correlation arises out of spectacular productivity increases in finance), the reported productivity of the financial sector is more of a statistical artefact. To see why, we can rearrange (3) and write:

$$P_i = \sigma_i^y \frac{P}{\sigma_i^e} \tag{4}$$

Since σ_i^y is increasing but σ_i^e is decreasing for the financial sector, its productivity based on standard national accounting is indeed too good to be true.

For comparison purposes, Table 4.4 shows data for thirty-three OECD countries in terms of the correlation between their value added and employment shares in finance and manufacturing, respectively. While manufacturing has, for the most part, a positive and statistically significant correlation between shares of output and employment (twenty-eight of thirty-three countries), in finance this is the exception rather than the rule (ten of thirty-two countries). The entries in italics indicate no statistical significance, whereas the entries in bold indicate negative correlation.

4.3 Output and final use-value

Given this logic as well as the observed patterns, the next question is, do financial services have a final output at all? The standard national

Table 4.4 Coefficients of correlation between shares of value added and shares of employment, finance vs. manufacturing, OECD countries, 1987–2009

	Finance		*Manufacturing*	
	correlation	*p-value*	*correlation*	*p-value*
Australia	**−0.75**	0.00	0.98	0.00
Austria	0.74	0.00	0.73	0.00
Belgium	0.09	*0.70*	0.96	0.00
Canada	0.17	*0.40*	0.51	0.02
Czech Republic	0.21	*0.46*	0.67	0.00
Denmark	0.04	*0.86*	0.98	0.00
Finland	0.56	0.01	0.56	0.01
France	0.83	0.00	0.98	0.00
Germany	0.50	0.01	0.92	0.00
Estonia	0.52	0.03	0.64	0.01
Greece	0.41	*0.13*	0.88	0.00
Hungary	0.32	*0.20*	0.05	*0.85*
Iceland	0.32	*0.20*	0.87	0.00
Ireland	0.81	0.00	0.56	0.01
Israel	0.73	0.02	0.66	*0.05*
Italy	**−0.28**	*0.20*	0.96	0.00
Japan	**−0.57**	0.01	0.96	0.00
Korea	0.25	*0.11*	0.21	*0.33*
Luxembourg	0.75	0.00	0.98	0.00
Mexico	0.51	*0.06*	0.31	*0.26*
Netherlands	**−0.17**	*0.44*	0.98	0.00
New Zealand	**−0.19**	*0.45*	0.97	0.00
Norway	0.83	0.00	0.96	0.00
Poland	0.31	*0.26*	0.87	0.00
Portugal			0.97	0.00
Slovak Republic	**−0.72**	0.00	0.63	0.01
Slovenia	**−0.44**	*0.10*	0.90	0.00
Spain	0.17	*0.44*	0.97	0.00
Sweden	**−0.73**	0.00	0.68	0.00
Switzerland	**−0.44**	*0.07*	0.73	0.00
Turkey	0.87	0.00	**−0.78**	0.01
United Kingdom	**−0.69**	0.00	0.99	0.00
United States	**−0.41**	0.05	0.99	0.00

Source: OECD STAN database

accounts answer in the affirmative, and treat finance like any other sector. Specifically, as mentioned above, value added in the financial sector is calculated in the same way as it is for other industries:

$$VA = Y - IC \tag{5}$$

where Y is imputed based on the sum of fee-based revenues of financial institutions and IC is imputed based on their related costs (making "value added" in this case nothing more than an imputation based on financial profits from fee-based services). Basu and Foley's NFVA indicator, meanwhile, leaves out this "value added" on the assumption that it is not measurable and thus cannot be linked to generating aggregate demand.[5]

Should finance be included in or excluded from total value added? And what happens when a commodity does not have a final use-value, that is, what if it cannot be used in final consumption? As mentioned above, money cannot be consumed directly, but merely serves to purchase other goods and services which are then used (in either intermediate or final consumption). It can therefore not be considered an output (for final consumption), implying there is no value added from selling money. Thus, we cannot use the VA = Y − IC formula as in other industries. Should we exclude the imputed financial "value added" then, as Basu and Foley do?

Financial services, however, are paid for by households and firms. Thus, financial revenues (from which financial "output" is imputed) are not simply non-productive for the economy – they represent an opportunity cost (similar to the SNA treatment of dwelling-owning households as described above) in that the money paid for them could have been spent on productive activities elsewhere. This, coupled with the observed negative correlation between finance's shares in output and employment, suggests that the sector is extractive rather than productive (or value-reducing rather than value-adding). It is therefore more accurate to account for the financial sector as a cost of producing the rest of GDP, that is, a cost involved in generating all true value added. In other words, the "output" of finance should be deducted, not merely excluded, from GDP as it is the ultimate and ubiquitous intermediate input (albeit an intermediate cost rather than an input for intermediate consumption) to all industries producing a use-value output of either goods or services.

This methodology goes beyond the SNA 53 approach, which merely treated finance as non-productive. Also, while novel, it builds on two elements already existing in SNA 68 and SNA 93. From SNA 68 it takes the concept of applying the output (not value added) of the financial sector as an input with a negative sign, though in our proposed measure it is an input to the rest of the economy rather than to an imaginary sector; it also mirrors the treatment recommended for the FISIM income by SNA 93, applied symmetrically to the fee-based part of financial incomes. Recall that FISIM in SNA 93 is distributed to uses, so several industries that pay for financial services show a lower value added than they would otherwise. This clearly shows that the amount of revenue received by financial institutions is a cost of production to other sectors. Applying this logic to the fee-based (non-FISIM) part of financial incomes (in the aggregate) would mean deducting the total revenue of financial transactions (from which financial "output" is imputed) from the total value added in the economy, making the treatment of all financial activities in the SNA consistent.

We believe that both the standard national accounts and the NFVA/NMVA indexes overestimate the contribution of finance to GDP and therefore overstate GDP in the process. The NFVA/NMVA method excludes only the value added of finance and not its total output (revenue) from the measure; recall that according to (5) above, VA = Y − IC, which can be rearranged to show that output is the sum of value added and intermediate consumption (Y = VA + IC). By leaving out only the VA part of finance, NFVA/NMVA leaves in the income stream for the intermediate consumption of financial institutions themselves, resulting in double counting. Standard GDP errs twice, first in failing to net out financial output (revenue) as a cost, and again in adding financial "value added" to total value added.

The approach proposed here, then, differs from the NFVA/NMVA framework in three ways. First, it does not stop at excluding the value added imputed to finance but additionally gives its (imputed) total "output" a negative sign since it is a cost of producing all other value added in the economy. Second, it does not exclude other sectors for which value added is imputed. The reasoning here is that such sectors, e.g. government, education, health, etc., do provide very concrete final use-value (in the form of defense, law and order, instruction, medical care) and thus have final outputs. Their measurement is indeed a contested issue as there is no independent measure of their output, but unlike finance, these sectors do not merely transfer exchange value, they actually produce final use-value, measurable or not. This logic is also based on the fact that education, health, and government services all produce employment-intensive tangible services, such as classes taught, medical checkups and surgeries, and military and police activities. The greater the volume of such services produced, the more employment is required to carry them out. In finance, however, the core activities involve managing, transferring, and repackaging money in ever more ingenious ways. A financial firm handling $1 billion in assets with 100 employees will not need to hire 900 more staff if its asset base increases to $10 billion (as can be seen from the correlation shown in Table 4.3).

Third and finally, Basu and Foley compare their measures of value added (either narrow measured of non-financial) to standard GDP measures, but as mentioned above, GDP includes taxes net of subsidies while value added does not. Our approach will thus adjust the proposed final use-value added measure to derive final GDP.

Overall, then, the role of finance in the total economy can be treated as follows:

$$VA_{\theta} = \Sigma\,(Y_i - IC_i) - Y_{\varphi} \qquad (6)$$

where θ stands for the total economy, i for each of the industries *other* than finance, and ϕ for the financial sector. This measure can be called final value added (FVA), as it applies the value added formula to all sectors producing output that has a final use-value, while deducting the "output" of finance (which only transfers exchange value) as a cost (or intermediate input) to the total economy. Once again, this is similar to what SNA 93 recommends for the FISIM part of financial incomes, even as it neglects to treat the fee-based incomes of the sector similarly (applying the standard value added formula instead).

Put another way, standard GDP mixes in a cost of production (finance) with its net output (value added for all other sectors), providing an illusion of business as usual, while FGDP (Final GDP: FVA plus taxes minus subsidies) – deducting financial costs from economic value creation – shows a more somber and realistic picture of where the economy is and where it may be going. In fact, in this sense GDP is even less consistent than Skousen's gross output measure mentioned above. The latter consistently includes all intermediate sales from one firm to another (Colander 2014, 453). Colander points out that Gross Output (GO) is really a measure of market activity rather than of output, and proposes renaming it gross domestic market activity (GDMA). Nonetheless, it is a consistent measure of such activity in that it applies the rule of including intermediate sales to all sectors. GDP, by contrast, gives finance a special treatment even though it has no final use-value. Instead of netting it out as it does with other intermediate inputs, GDP counts it as output. FGDP is thus an adjustment symmetrical but opposite to that of Skousen. It is the demand-side equivalent of GO, in that it consistently does not include any intermediate transactions in the calculation of value added (with finance treated like any other intermediate input), and thus measures only final output, that is, output that has final use-value and is available for final consumption by households or government. Put another way, GO includes all intermediate inputs, GDP mixes an intermediate input (finance) with net outputs (value added), and FGDP counts only final, net outputs. This is shown schematically in Figure 4.2.

Figure 4.2 A schematic comparison of FGDP, GDP, and GO

4.4 Empirical estimates of FGDP

We now look at data on financial services in the US, one of the most financialized economies in the OECD, "with more than 30% of [its] value added coming from the financial sector" (Assa, 2012, 36). Data were taken from the United Nations Main Aggregates and Detailed Tables (MADT) database, rather than from the Bureau of Economic Analysis. An international source ensures higher comparability between countries and across time than a national statistical source. Furthermore, the UN's MADT database has historical records of national accounts data in different SNA systems – SNA 68, SNA 93, and, for a few countries, SNA 2008. This is useful (as shown above) for distinguishing different treatments of finance in different countries and at different times.

For the United States, data on the FIRE sector in the MADT database begin in 1977. We look at data from MADT table 202 – value added by industries at constant prices. The use of constant (rather than current) prices in this dataset ensures that we are looking at real value added and real GDP and not their nominal equivalents (available in table 201 of the UN database). Looking at a cross section of GDP by value added, Table 4.5 presents the data for 2011, in 1985 prices (based on SNA 93).

As mentioned above, the difference between value added and GDP is equal to taxes net of subsidies on products (as well as a statistical discrepancy). According to this table, finance accounted for 26.6 percent of all total value added in the US in 2011 (row 9), $2.1 trillion out of a total of $7.8 trillion (in 1985 dollars). Using the NFVA approach (row 16 = row 13 − row 9), total value added comes to only $5.7 trillion, or 73 percent of its standard equivalent. The NMVA measure (row 16 = row 13 − rows 9 through 12) would yield $4.5 trillion, or 57 percent of the mainstream figure.

In order to compare these numbers to the FVA measure, which not only excludes the "value added" of the FIRE sector but also deducts its "output," the data from MADT table 202 are not sufficient, since they give only the value added for the FIRE sector (calculated as

Table 4.5 Breakdown of value added for the United States, 2011, in 1985 prices and as a percentage of total value added

Line	*Industry*	*1985 million dollars*	*% of value added*
1	Agriculture, hunting, forestry; fishing	161,642	2.1%
2	Mining and quarrying	124,714	1.6%
3	Manufacturing	1,502,866	19.3%
4	Electricity, gas, and water supply	200,009	2.6%
5	Construction	173,282	2.2%
6	Wholesale, retail trade, repair of motor vehicles, motorcycles, and personal and household goods; hotels and restaurants	1,585,951	20.4%
7	Hotels and restaurants	74,670	1.0%
8	Transport, storage, and communications	695,527	8.9%
9	Financial intermediation, real estate, renting, and business activities	2,073,814	26.6%
10	Public administration and defense; compulsory social security	630,269	8.1%
11	Education; health and social work; other community, social, and personal services	621,654	8.0%
12	Private households with employed persons	9,552	0.1%
13	Equals: VALUE ADDED, GROSS, in basic prices	7,789,051	100.0%
14	Equals: GROSS DOMESTIC PRODUCT	7,762,152	99.7%
15	NFVA (= 13–9)	5,715,237	73.4%
16	NMVA (= 13–9–10–11–12)	4,453,762	57.2%
17	FIRE output	3,226,692	41.4%
18	FVA (= 13–9–17)	2,488,545	31.9%
19	GDP/value added	0.9965	
20	FGDP (= 18*19)	2,479,951	31.8%

Source: United Nations Main Aggregates and Detailed Tables (MADT) database

output − intermediate consumption). To get the data for output before intermediate consumption is deducted from it, table 203 of the MADT database was used. While this table is in current prices, it can be used to calculate the proportion of output to value added in each year since both variables are in the same prices. For example, reported financial output in the United States for 2011 was $7.736 trillion. From this, $2.764 trillion of intermediate consumption is deducted to arrive at value added of $4.972 trillion, meaning the ratio of output to value added in 2011 was 7.736/4.972 = 1.56 (or, conversely, value added was 1/1.56 of output, i.e. 64 percent). Applying this to our constant price data of $2.1 trillion we get financial output in constant prices (for 2011) of $3.2 trillion. Deducting this figure from the reported 2011 total value added gives total final value added of $2.489 trillion, or 44 percent of standard value added. Thus the FVA measure ends up below both NFVA and NMVA, as a percentage of standard value added. As mentioned above, however, to be consistent with the other three approaches to GDP, value added must be adjusted by adding taxes and subtracting subsidies. In 2011 the reported ratio of GDP to value added was 0.9965, so applying this to our FVA measure yields FGDP of $2.480 trillion (compared with $13.2 trillion in the official figure). This calculation (as well as those involved in deriving GDP from value added, NFGDP from NFVA and NMGDP from NMVA) is carried out in Table 4.6.

Applying the FGDP method to a longer time series, Figure 4.3 demonstrates that the various alternative measures are indeed narrower than standard GDP in official national accounts. Note that FGDP is lower than NMGDP even though the former includes more sectors than the latter. This is because FGDP deducts a larger amount – the gross "output" of finance from total value added, instead of just the net value added of finance – from total value added.

In addition to the different size of the US economy implied by Figure 4.3, there is a dramatic difference in the growth rates of the economy according to each measure. While GDP and NMGDP show a cumulative growth of 82 percent and 84 percent over the period 1987–2011, respectively, NFGDP suggests a more moderate increase of 74 percent, with FGDP far more pessimistic at 34 percent. By comparison, total nonfarm employment grew by 29.1 percent over the same period, strengthening the case for FGDP as a more realistic measure of real net output.

Furthermore, FGDP has the lowest mean growth rate and highest standard deviation of all measures (see Table 4.7). This is in line with our theory of finance as having a negative contribution to total output.

Table 4.6 Value added and GDP for the United States in 2011 (millions of 1985 dollars) using four approaches

	Standard	*Non-financial*	*Narrow measured*	*Final use-value*
Initial value added (total economy)	7,789,051	7,789,051	7,789,051	7,789,051
1. Deduct value added of finance (and other imputed sectors in NMVA*)		−2,073,814	−3,335,289	−2,073,814
2. Deduct gross output of finance				**−3,226,692**
New value added	7,789,051	5,715,237	4,453,762	2,488,545
Taxes minus subsidies factor	0.9965	0.9965	0.9965	0.9965
GDP equivalent	7,762,152	5,695,500	4,438,381	2,479,951

* Financial intermediation, real estate, renting, and business activities; public administration and defense; compulsory social security; education; health and social work; other community, social, and personal services; private households with employed persons.

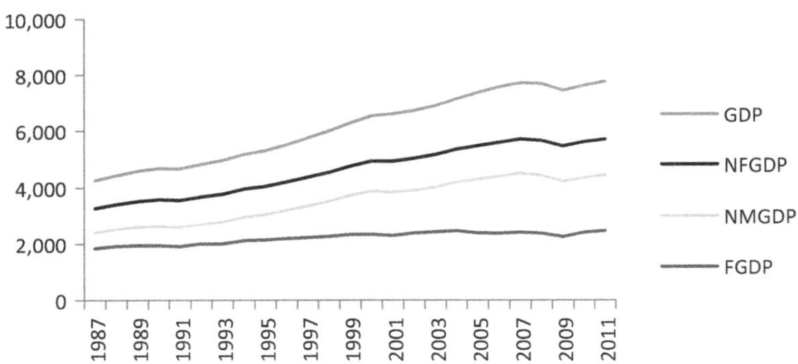

Figure 4.3 Levels of GDP, non-financial GDP, narrow-measured GDP, and usable GDP, in billions of 1985 dollars

Table 4.7 Mean and standard deviation of growth rates using GDP, NMGDP, NFGDP, and FGDP

	GDP	*NFGDP*	*NMGDP*	*FGDP*
Mean growth rate	2.6%	2.3%	2.6%	1.3%
Standard deviation	1.8%	2.0%	2.6%	2.8%

It also foreshadows a discussion of finance smoothing over volatility in the rest of the economy (see next chapter).

4.5 Conclusion

This chapter discussed the inconsistent treatment of financial income in the national accounts. Interest-based financial intermediation is considered to be an input to other industries. Thus this income is deducted from the value added of the consuming industries, while the whole amount of financial intermediation services is netted out of value added to arrive at GDP. Fee-based financial services, however, are imputed a value added based on net income, and show up on the output side of the accounts like any regular industry.

We have argued that this is wrong, both conceptually and empirically. First, finance – whether fee based or not – does not provide a final use-value, but is rather a provision of exchange value. At most it can be seen as having intermediate use-value, as an input to other industries. Empirically, financial services have a negative correlation between their shares of total value added and their shares of total employment, presenting a paradox of seemingly negative productivity. To resolve these logical and measurement issues, we propose a new measure – final gross domestic product – which treats financial fee income in the same way that net financial interest flows are currently treated in the national accounts. We deduct the total output of the financial sector from aggregate value added since it is a cost of other industries (and the economy as a whole). The resulting series is the demand-side mirror of Skousen's gross output, in that the former consistently nets out all intermediate consumption, while the latter consistently includes it.

The appendix to this chapter explores the implications of this output-side adjustment for the expenditure and income sides of the accounts. In this we also follow the example of standard national accounting, and use the cases of commuting costs and employer-provided medical services as models. Financial services provided for a fee are reclassified in our FGDP framework from final consumption expenditure to intermediate consumption, thus reducing total expenditure as well as value added. On the income side, the relative shares of wages, taxes, and profits in the financial sector are applied to the total deduction amount in order to remove this component from total income. Since the income structure of the financial sector is profit heavy, this adjustment results in a higher wage share and lower profit share in the revised view of the economy through FGDP. The final two chapters explore the implications of these adjustments to the overall structure and dynamics of the economy.

Appendix 4.A Reconciling FGDP with the income and expenditure sides of national accounts

The discussion above presented an alternative measure of output, FGDP, based on the value added approach and treating finance as an economic cost rather than an employment-creating output. The analysis would not be complete, however, without looking at what this new measure of production implies for the other two approaches in national accounting, that is, the income and expenditure sides. This is because, in principle, all three aggregates – GDP by the income, product, and expenditure approaches – must match since they are all accounting identities. In practice, however, there is often a statistical discrepancy due to the fact that each estimate relies on different data sources.[6]

4.A.1 Rationale

As we have seen, FGDP is a measure of net output, which treats financial output as an intermediate input and therefore deducts it from total value added (as well as excluding the value added imputed to the financial sector). This procedure is based on two arguments: conceptually, it rests on the assumption that finance (and its core product, money or credit) has no final use-value; empirically, it builds on the negative correlation found between the share of finance in total output and its share in total employment. Incomes generated in the financial sector, however, remain on income side of the accounts, and likewise are equal to someone's expenditures. At this stage, and as a basis for adjusting the income and expenditure aggregates in line with the FGDP idea, it is useful to look at how the SNA treats two other services which have both intermediate and final consumption elements: commuting to work and employment-related medical exams.

Regarding commuting, the 1993 SNA has the following instruction:

> The following types of goods and services provided to employees must be treated as part of intermediate consumption: ... Transportation and hotel services provided while the employee is travelling on business.
>
> (SNA 1993, 6.155)

The 2008 SNA likewise states the following:

> Services provided to employees carrying out their tasks, for example the cost of food and hotel accommodation when travelling on

> business, is treated as intermediate consumption of the employer and not final consumption of the employee.
>
> (SNA 2008, 8.99)

Furthermore, SNA 2008 also stipulates:

> The following types of goods and services provided to employees must be treated as part of intermediate consumption: ... Transportation and hotel services including allowances for meals provided while the employee is travelling on business ... First aid facilities, medical examinations or other health checks required because of the nature of the work ... Employees may sometimes be responsible for purchasing the kinds of goods or services listed above and be subsequently reimbursed in cash by the employer. Such cash reimbursements must be treated as intermediate expenditures by the employer and not as part of the employee's wages and salaries.
>
> (SNA 2008, 6.222)

It is interesting to note that in both versions of the SNA, the treatment of work-related travel and health services depends on whether the employer or the employee pays for them. In the former case, they are considered business costs and counted as intermediate consumption (on the output side of GDP); in the latter, they are treated as personal consumption and counted as final consumption expenditure (on the expenditure side of GDP).

The implications of whether these services are classified as intermediate consumption inputs or as final consumption expenditures can be illustrated by a simple example. Assume an economy consists of only one large firm, producing $1 million worth of gross output, of which $600,000 is intermediate consumption, leaving value added of $400,000. Ignoring for the moment the net taxes difference between value added and GDP, this implies total income and expenditure of $400,000 as well (i.e. GDP = $400,000 by all three approaches). At an initial period, say T_0, the costs of commuting and work-related medical exams (which amount to $100,000 each year) are paid for by the workers, not the firms, and are thus included under the $400,000 GDP by expenditure side.

Suppose further that after the end of the first year, in T_1, firms start paying for these services, relieving the workers of the burden of paying these costs. Table 4.8A shows how this change impacts overall GDP in the economy in all three measures.

Table 4.8A Impact on GDP of changing the treatment of commuting and medical exams

GDP by production	T_0	T_1	*GDP by expenditure*	T_0	T_1	*GDP by income*	T_0	T_1
Gross output	$1,000,000	$1,000,000	Consumption	$200,000	$100,000	Profits	$150,000	$50,000
Less: Intermediate consumption	$600,000	$700,000	Plus: I+G+X−M	$200,000	$200,000	Plus: Wages and net taxes	$250,000	$250,000
Equals: **Value added**	**$400,000**	**$300,000**	*Equals:* **Total expenditure**	**$400,000**	**$300,000**	*Equals:* **Total income**	**$400,000**	**$300,000**

Reclassifying the $100,000 cost of commuting or work-related medical services from the final consumption of workers to an intermediate consumption of firms has three effects: reducing value added by $100,000 (since value added = gross output − intermediate consumption, and the latter has been increased by $100,000); reducing total expenditure by $100,000 (since final consumption expenditure is now lower by $100,000, with the other parts – G, I, and X and M – unchanged); and reducing profits, taxes and wages by $100,000 (since profits = revenues − costs, and business costs have just risen by $100,000). In all three measures, GDP has gone down from $400,000 to $300,000, simply because of the reclassification of the services under question.

Why does the SNA allow multiple ways to treat the same service (commuting or work-related medical exams) depending on who pays for it? Empirically, one explanation could be that it would be more difficult to attribute such costs to consumers than to firms. At a more conceptual level, however, this may be explained either by a neoclassical appeal to the idea of workers spending on contributions to their human capital, or more reasonably by the fact that the activities in question can be undertaken both by consumers in their free time and by workers in work-related situations. That is, these services have both a final use (for personal consumption) and an intermediate use (as an input or intermediate cost of production), depending on the context. This is explained by the SNA as follows:

> An employer, whether government or not, may provide an employee with equipment that is necessary to carrying out the labor services the employee provides. Examples are uniforms or small tools, such as scissors for hairdressers or bicycles for delivering mail. This equipment is recorded as intermediate consumption of the employing enterprise and is never recorded as being acquired by the household to which the employee belongs. The same convention applies to services provided to employees carrying out their tasks.
>
> (SNA 2008, 8.99)

But does this logic apply to financial services? SNA 2008 implies that it does. A section dealing with charging for financial services reads as follows:

> Explicit fees should always be recorded as payable by the unit to whom the services are rendered to the institution performing the service. If the services are rendered to a corporation or to government, the costs will form part of intermediate consumption. If they

> are rendered to households they will be treated as final consumption unless the financial service is performed in relation to an unincorporated enterprise, including the owning and occupying of a dwelling.
>
> (SNA 2008, 17.234)

This is similar to the commute and medical-exam cases, in that the classification of the services is based on who is paying, i.e. the SNA allocates fee-based financial incomes based on whether the buyer of these services is a household, on the one hand, or firms and government, on the other hand. The implication is that fee-based services provided to the latter are already netted out as intermediate input, while services provided to households (except in their capacity as home-owners) show up on the expenditure and income sides.

However, there is a gross inconsistency here. In both the commute and work-related medical exam cases, it is a firm (the employer) either paying for services consumed by its employees (in which case these services show up as intermediate consumption) or not paying (in which case the employees pay and the services show up as final consumption expenditure). In contrast, financial services to corporations and governments are services paid for by one firm to another, rather than by a firm for its employees. This asymmetry (firm to firm vs. firm to employees) has political economy implications. When financial corporations deal with non-financial corporations, "there is scope for systematic mutual gains in arm's-length relationships" between them (dos Santos, 2009, 16), while the relationship between financial firms and individuals or households is far more unequal (ibid., 12).

Furthermore, as explained above, financial services to individuals or households are not final (having no direct use-value) and therefore should not be considered as final consumption. Even outside of financing mortgages (for owner-occupier households), financial services such as student loans, car loans, and even credit cards are not services producing a final consumable output. What these services do is provide households with the money they need to purchase other goods and services, such as an education, a car, or groceries. Finance is therefore mediating between borrowing households' current incomes and consumption needs. On the saving side, finance can be seen as offering savers a form of deferred consumption (similar to what Keynes advocated in his 1940 book *How to Pay for the War*), once again not current final consumption. More broadly, in terms of aggregate demand analysis, finance falls into the same pool of leakages as savings, taxes, and imports – which are offset only by injections of demand from investment, government spending, and exports – because it diverts spending away from current consumption on other, final goods and services to paying financing fees.

For all these reasons, the "output" of fee-based financial services – imputed as mentioned above from their gross revenues – needs to be deducted from GDP by expenditure – since the expenditure is not on a final good or service – and from GDP by income – since finance is an intermediate cost of firms and therefore a deduction from their gross profits. The amount to be deducted, as demonstrated on the output side, is equal to imputed "output" as well as the "value added" of the FIRE sectors, around $7.5 trillion in 2013 (in 2009 dollars).

4.A.2 Reconciling FGDP on the expenditure side

The adjustment on the expenditure side is less straightforward than on the output side, since we need to look at the contribution of each sector to the four categories of expenditure: final consumption expenditure (FCE), gross fixed capital formation (GFCF, which is the sum of fixed investment and changes in inventories), government expenditure (G) and net exports (NX = exports minus imports). This requires the use of input–output tables, as seen in Table 4.9A which shows the distribution of GDP by expenditure for 2012 from the input–output table.

As Table 4.9A shows, government spending appears as one of the expenditure sectors (second column from the right), but the input-output analysis does not show it as a recipient of financial value added. Therefore, its expenditure in our adjustment was kept constant, while the other three components – FCE, GFCF, and NX – have been reduced proportionally to the share of financial value added coming from them.

In 2012, the bulk of expenditure on fee-based financial services, 93 percent, was attributed to personal consumption expenditure (which matches the SNA recommendation), 3 percent to private fixed investment, 5 percent to exports, and 2 percent to imports (that is, −2 percent in the accounting). The total deduction[7] (amounting to 49.3 percent of GDP, the sum of financial value added and financial output) could be proportionally subtracted from the above-mentioned sectors. Denoting the total amount to be deducted by F, Table 4.10A shows the steps in the calculation.

As we can see by comparing columns (b) and (f), the distribution of GDP by expenditure categories changes dramatically between GDP and FGDP. The dynamics and meaning of this difference will be discussed in detail in the next chapter.

Table 4.9A Input–output contribution of each sector to expenditure categories of GDP

	FCE	*GFCF*	*G*	*NX*
Agriculture, forestry, fishing, and hunting	103%	−15%	0%	12%
Mining	0%	−78%	0%	178%
Utilities	100%	0%	0%	0%
Construction	0%	69%	31%	0%
Manufacturing	91%	39%	6%	−36%
Wholesale trade	53%	20%	2%	24%
Retail trade	96%	4%	0%	0%
Transportation and warehousing	64%	8%	1%	27%
Information	70%	20%	1%	9%
Finance, insurance, real estate, rental, and leasing	***93%***	***3%***	***0%***	***3%***
Professional and business services	21%	54%	18%	6%
Educational services, health care, and social assistance	100%	0%	0%	0%
Arts, entertainment, recreation, accommodation, and food services	99%	0%	0%	0%
Other services, except government	101%	0%	0%	−1%
Government	3%	0%	97%	0%

Source: Data from table "The use of commodities by industries, before redefinitions (producers' prices)," BEA

4.A.3 Reconciling FGDP on the income side

The commuting and work-related medical issues in the SNA discussed above pointed to an explicit link in the national accounts between the expenditure and output sides. The link is consumption, which has two stages – intermediate and final. An activity that is classified as intermediate consumption falls on the output side and is netted out of gross output (to arrive at value added); otherwise it is treated as final consumption and shows up on the expenditure side. The input–output tables also facilitate this connection between output and expenditure, since they show how the output of each industry (row) is separated out by expenditure sector (i.e. 93 percent of financial value added, as we have seen above, is attributed to final consumption expenditure).

Reconciliation on the income side is more complicated. First, we lack a conceptual bridge between income and output, similar to the role consumption serves between output and expenditure. Second, and more importantly for our purposes here, the input–output tables show only the breakdown by income – to wages, taxes, and profits – at the bottom of the table, i.e. on the input side. In other words, the columns – which represent

Table 4.10A Adjusting GDP on the expenditure side, US data for 2012

Item	*GDP*		*Shares of financial value added*	*FGDP*		
	*Millions of dollars**	*% of total*		*Deduction*	*Millions of dollars**	*% of total*
	(a)	*(b)*	*(c)*	*(d) = (c)* F*	*(e) = (a) – (d)*	*(f)*
GDP by expenditure	16,245	100.0%	100.0%	F = 8,004	8,240	100.0%
Personal consumption expenditures	11,150	68.6%	93.4%	7,474	3,676	44.6%
Government consumption expenditures	3,167	19.5%	N.A.	N.A.	3,167	38.4%
Gross private domestic investment	2,475	15.2%	3.2%	258	2,217	26.9%
Net exports	−547	−3.4%	3.4%	273	−820	−9.9%

* The input–output tables are presented in current dollars for each year. Therefore, the calculations were done in current dollars to get the adjusted percentages.

industries and their inputs in the input–output tables – have three additional cells after all the commodities serving as input for the given industry, and these show the breakdown of wages, taxes, and profits in that sector, e.g. in finance. Thus we can see that, in 2012, 24 percent of the income in the financial sector consisted of wages, 9 percent was taxes less subsidies, and 68 percent on profits. As Table 4.11A shows, the FIRE sector is one of the three top industries in terms of share of income going to profits, along with agriculture and mining, which are also the three industries with the lowest share of wages in their income (less than 25).

How does this help us reconcile the FGDP adjustment, made on the output side, with the income side of national accounts (Table 4.12A)? The most straightforward methodology would be to apply the relative shares of wages, taxes, and profits in the financial sector to the total deduction (denoted F as above), and thus distribute the adjustment proportionally to the income categories of the whole economy.

Once again, as on the expenditure side, the application of the FGDP adjustment to the income side results in different relative shares of income. In this case, the results are quite dramatic, with the wage share[8] going up from 53.1 percent of GDP to 81.7 percent of FGDP, while gross profits decreased from 40.4 percent of GDP to a mere 13.9 percent

Table 4.11A Income breakdown of each sector of GDP

	Compensation of employees	*Taxes on production and imports, less subsidies*	*Gross operating surplus*	*Total*
Agriculture, forestry, fishing, and hunting	21%	1%	77%	100%
Mining	21%	10%	69%	100%
Utilities	26%	22%	52%	100%
Construction	64%	1%	35%	100%
Manufacturing	46%	3%	51%	100%
Wholesale trade	48%	20%	32%	100%
Retail trade	55%	21%	24%	100%
Transportation and warehousing	58%	6%	35%	100%
Information	35%	5%	60%	100%
Finance, insurance, real estate, rental, and leasing	***24%***	***9%***	***68%***	***100%***
Professional and business services	71%	2%	26%	100%
Educational services, health care, and social assistance	83%	3%	14%	100%
Arts, entertainment, recreation, accommodation, and food services	62%	12%	26%	100%
Other services, except government	71%	5%	23%	100%
Government	80%	−1%	21%	100%

Source: Data from table "The use of commodities by industries, before redefinitions (producers' prices)," BEA

of FGDP. While both categories have been reduced in absolute terms in the adjustment process, gross profits were reduced far more (as explained above, due to the large share of profits in financial value added, 67.7 percent, compared with wages' share of 23.6 percent).

It is now clear how the treatment of finance as an intermediate input will affect all three measures of GDP. Net output or value added – GDP(O) – will be reduced by treating finance as a cost (intermediate input) rather than an output; likewise, total expenditure – GDP(E) – will go down since no final expenditure on finance will be registered; finally, total income – GDP(I) – will go down as well, with profits declining more than wages, as per the income structure of the financial sector, which is now treated as an overall cost to the economy. Figure 4.4A presents the adjustment between the three approaches schematically.

Table 4.12A Adjusting GDP on the income side, US data for 2012

Item	*GDP*		*Shares of financial value added*	*FGDP*		
	*Millions of dollars**	*% of total*		*Deduction*	*Millions of dollars**	*% of total*
	(a)	*(b)*	*(c)*	*(d) = (c)* F*	*(e) = (a) − (d)*	*(f)*
GDP by income	16,245	100.0%	100.0%	F = 8,004	8,240	100.0%
Compensation of employees	8,620	53.1%	23.6%	1,887	6,733	81.7%
Taxes on production and imports, less subsidies	1,066	6.6%	8.8%	702	364	4.4%
Gross operating surplus	6,559	40.4%	67.7%	5,416	1,143	13.9%

* The input–output tables are presented in current dollars for each year. Therefore, the calculations were done in current dollars to get the adjusted percentages.

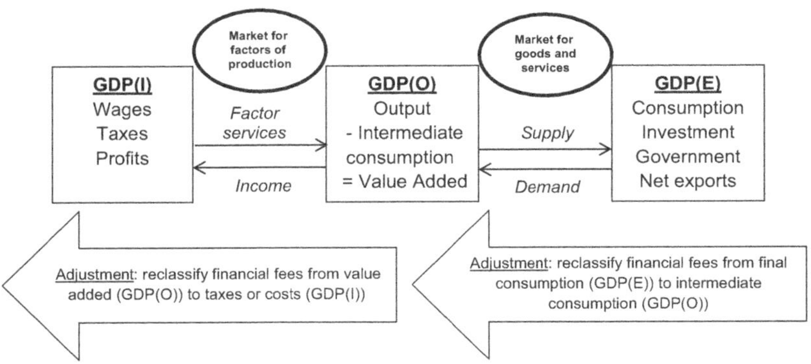

Figure 4.4A Reconciliation of the three approaches to GDP

Notes

1 Christophers (2011) describes in detail how what is deemed productive, formally known as the production boundary of national accounts, has shifted dramatically over time, especially with regards to financial services. For constructive critiques of the mainstream placement of the production boundary, see Shaikh and Tonak (1994) and Basu and Foley (2013).
2 The data in Table 4.2 are for 1996, the last year for which data were reported according to both SNA 68 and SNA 93 for the United States.
3 Not all production is undertaken by enterprises. For example, dwelling-owning households are considered to be producing housing services for themselves, the imputation of which is included in GDP and is equal to the rents they would otherwise pay (reflecting their opportunity cost).
4 Goldman Sachs CEO Lloyd Blankfein was quoted by the *Financial Times* as saying, in March of 2010, that "the people of Goldman Sachs are among the most productive in the world" (*Huffington Post*, 2010).
5 Basu and Foley (2013) focus more specifically on the question of the discrepancy between indices of output and employment, rather than trying to develop an aggregate that consistently represents the contribution of various sectors to net output, as is the case here.
6 Rosnick and Baker (2011) estimate the size of the discrepancy at around 0.5 percent of GDP between 1947 and 2011, and explain the phenomenon based on misclassification of short-term capital gains as ordinary income. Another explanation is provided by Thoma (2005), who links the discrepancies to the share of government in output.
7 Notice that we are again adding up the value added and the output of the FIRE sector, as in the previous chapter. By applying the proportion of FIRE *value added* to this larger figure, however, we are making an assumption that the same proportions apply to FIRE *output*, which may not be correct. In the absence of further data, however, this estimate will have to suffice.
8 Compensation of employees includes not only wages, to be precise, but also benefits.

5 GDP on FIRE

Financialization, stagnation, and leakages from aggregate demand

> To understand the operation of the system, one figure is not enough. You want to see how it disaggregates.
>
> (Wassily Leontief, interviewed by Duncan Foley, April 14, 1997)

5.1 The need for a better aggregate

The three weaknesses of GDP discussed in the introduction to this book – its failure as a leading indicator, its divergence from measures of employment, and its decoupling from median income – beg two questions: first, what caused the deterioration[1] in the indicative power of GDP, both as a leading indicator and as a proxy for aggregate demand and standard of living (at least in the economic sense of the word)? Second, does the flawed nature of GDP require the use of a more complex set of data, e.g. input–output tables (as the quote above from Leontief suggests) or the dash-board approach (to use Fleurbaey and Blanchet's (2013) term) – i.e. the need to rely on multiple data sources or series for a clear picture of aggregate demand – or can a revised aggregate such as FGDP still convey the missing information in one indicator? This chapter attempts to answer both questions.

As for the first, we document the financialization of economic activity in the United States, and examine how both the increasing reliance of the financial sector on consumer debt (instead of its traditional business lending model) and the standard treatment of financial fees as final expenditure may have made finance the soft underbelly of aggregate demand, covering up stagnationist or even recessionary tendencies. As for the second question, and building on the conceptual work done in the previous chapter, we analyze the relevance of the FGDP aggregate as an alternative to GDP. Specifically, we look at the real-world implications of our theory in relation to economic growth, aggregate demand, employment, distribution, disposable income, and the standard of living. Throughout the analysis we compare the performance of GDP with that of FGDP and evaluate their relative strength in helping us understand both current and past economic events, and their potential as leading indicators of future economic performance.

5.2 Financialization

The term "financialization" is normally used to refer to the increasing importance and proportion of financial activities, incomes, and profits in the economy, or a "pattern of accumulation in which profits accrue primarily through financial channels rather than through trade and commodity production" (Krippner, 2005). Various measures of this process include the size of the financial sector as a percentage of GDP (Assa, 2012, Kedrosky and Stangler, 2011), rentier income (interest and dividends) of non-financial corporations (Stockhammer, 2004), the financial sector's share of profits or the ratio of financial assets to GDP (Freeman, 2010), and portfolio income of non-financial firms as well as profits of financial versus non-financial firms (Krippner, 2005).

The literature also finds the process of financialization to be associated with stagnation or negative growth, inequality, and unemployment (Assa, 2012, Epstein, 2001, Freeman, 2010, Palley, 2007, Stockhammer, 2004, Yeldan, 2000). Different studies suggest different channels through which this negative impact occurs, but Stockhammer (2004) is typical in positing a shift in power from managers to shareholders, with a concomitant change of focus from the long-term growth of the firm to short-term profits (assuming a tradeoff between the two).

Like the studies cited in the introduction predicting the Great Recession, the literature on financialization uses a combination of GDP and non-GDP data. In both cases the incidence of financialization in advanced economies is clear. For example, in 1970 France and Mexico were the only two members of the OECD to report value added in finance exceeding 20 percent of GDP. This changed to twenty-eight of thirty-four members by 2008, including fifteen countries with more than 25 percent of GDP attributed to finance (recall that value added in finance, unlike the FISIM adjustment, includes only fee-based financial services which are more easily measured than interest differentials). In Australia, France, Israel, the UK, the US, and New Zealand, fee-based financial services accounted for more than 30 percent in GDP in 2008 (Assa, 2012).

Based on our previous discussion of the treatment of finance in national accounting, it becomes critical to understand what part of this process of financialization can be attributed to actual structural changes in the economy, and what part is due to methodological changes in accounting. As discussed in the previous chapter (and explained in detail in Christophers, 2011), the interest-based part of financial income has gone from being accounted for as non-productive (prior to 1953), to implicitly productive (between 1953 and 1993), to finally an explicitly productive activity in 1993. However, given that this part of finance affects only the *relative* size of the financial sector (and of industries paying for these interest differentials), it does not affect the overall level of GDP. The latter is impacted by the other type of financial income – fee-based services, which are imputed based on actual revenues (and costs) in finance. As Akritidis (2007) and dos Santos (2009) point out, this part of financial revenues was initially negligible, but had increased to nearly half of all incomes in finance by the first decade of the twenty-first century. Given that this income has been treated as an output in the national accounts since 1993, its increasing importance can weaken the link between GDP and aggregate demand, as will be shown below.

It is not a coincidence that finance, insurance, and real-estate activities are lumped together in the accounts as well as in the FIRE acronym. What these three types of activity have in common, in addition to their speculative nature, is that they generate incomes based on the creation, ownership, and trade of assets (financial, realty, or legal contracts) rather than production and trade of goods and services. Thus, even at the most fundamental level, they do not belong in a measure of production, but rather in balance sheets or flow of funds accounts.

One could say, then, that GDP itself – in addition to the actual economy it purports to measure – has become financialized. The next few sections analyze how the now-financialized GDP performs as a leading indicator, as well as a proxy for aggregate demand and the average standard of living. The analysis proceeds from several different angles, and compares GDP's performance to that of FGDP, its de-financialized version.

5.3 Volatility is alive and well: the Great Moderation as a statistical mirage

Beginning the analysis using real growth rates in quarterly frequency, Figure 5.1 compares GDP vs. FGDP based on quarterly data in 2009 dollars for the period 1987Q2–2013Q4 (BEA, NIPA).

Figure 5.2 shows the same information using a three-quarter moving average.

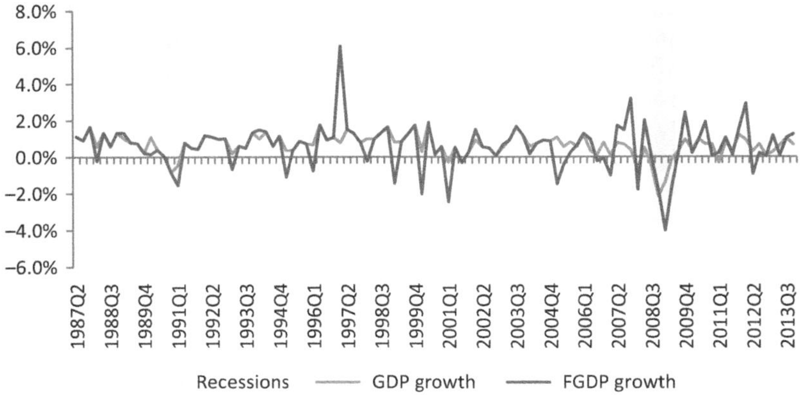

Figure 5.1 Quarterly growth rates of GDP vs. FGDP with NBER recessions shaded

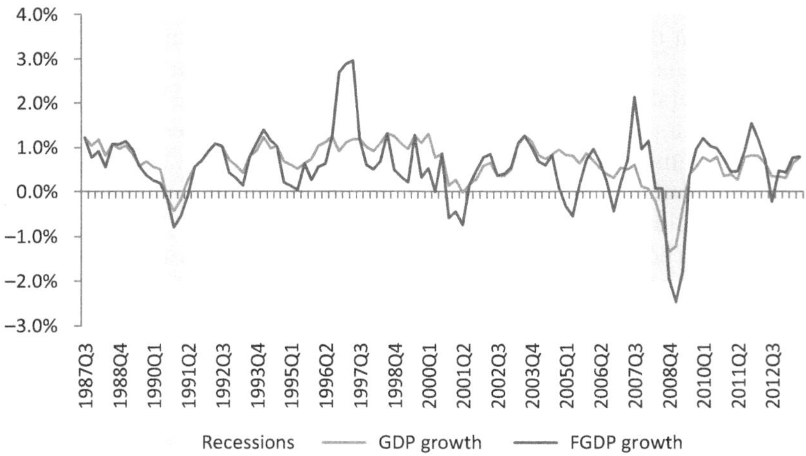

Figure 5.2 Growth rates of GDP vs. FGDP, three-quarter moving average with NBER recessions shaded

Looking at the figures, FGDP is clearly more volatile than GDP. While the two measures have the same mean growth rate (0.6 percent, either arithmetic or geometric), FGDP has a standard deviation of 1.2 percent compared with GDP's 0.6 percent. Furthermore, FGDP shows more pronounced spikes than GDP. For example, in the first quarter of 1997, FGDP has a high of 6.1 percent growth compared with a paltry 0.8 percent growth in GDP for the same quarter. The reason for this difference in volatility is the fact that GDP includes the less cyclically sensitive financial sector, masking the greater aggregate volatility of output visible in the FGDP series. This casts a doubt on the literature concerning the so-called "Great Moderation," which presumably began around 1993. Gali and Gambetti (2009), for example, explain this decline in volatility by pointing to several structural changes (rather than merely good luck), such as "shrinking contribution of non-technology shocks to output volatility ... a change in the interest rate rule, giving a larger weight to inflation stabilization (relative to output stabilization) and ... an apparent end of short run increasing returns to labor" (25–26). Likewise, Kim and Nelson (1999) explain the structural break in volatility by "a decline in the variance of shocks and a narrowing gap between growth rates during booms and recession" (615).

Crowley and Hallet (2014) already question this phenomenon by using wavelet and empirical mode decomposition analyses to show that volatility over this period had not vanished but rather moved from shorter (higher-frequency) cycles to longer (lower-frequency) ones. This analysis uses standard GDP and focuses on the composition of volatility based on this measure.

The problem, however, is that the financialization of GDP (the measure of output on which Crowley and Hallet depend) has implications for aggregate volatility, suggesting that the observation of a Great Moderation may be traced to still more fundamental measurement issues as described in the FGDP framework, and that the Great Moderation is ultimately a statistical mirage because of the mismeasurement of output, not a mere transfer of volatility from one frequency to another.

This idea is borne out by comparing the growth rate data of GDP vs. FGDP. Prior to 1993, the two measures have a similar standard deviation of growth (0.6 percent for GDP and 0.7 percent for FGDP, with a ratio of 0.78). From 1993 to 2013, GDP still has a standard deviation of 0.6 percent, while FGDP shows 1.3 percent instead (the ratio falling to 0.47). In other words, the Great Moderation, viewed in the lens of FGDP, is not a real macroeconomic phenomenon and therefore does not require explaining (or justifying).

5.4 GDP as a leading indicator

When it comes to the National Bureau of Economic Research (NBER) definition of recessions as at least two consecutive quarters of negative growth, Figure 5.2 above shows the same number and length of recessions using both GDP and FGDP (1990Q4–1991Q1 and 2008Q4–2009Q2). The depth of these recessions, however, is quite different, as demonstrated in Tables 5.1 and 5.2. In the first, two-quarter-long recession, GDP shows a contraction of output by −0.9 percent and −0.5 percent, while FGDP drops by −0.9 percent and −1.6 percent. The combined output loss is therefore 1.4 percent according to the standard measure, but 2.5 percent based on our adjusted indicator. Likewise, the second ("Great") recession shows up as a combined 3.7 percent drop in output in GDP, compared with 7.4 percent in FGDP. The latter measure also shows the Great Recession bottoming out with a −4.0 percent drop in 2009Q1, while GDP presents the bottom of the contraction a quarter earlier, in 2008Q4, with a mere −2.2 percent decline.

If we consider the three-quarter moving average chart, the period 2000Q4–2001Q2 appears as a small recession, with FGDP growth rates of −0.6 percent, −0.4 percent, and −0.7 percent (a combined −1.8 percent contraction), whereas GDP shows no recession in this timeframe. The length of the Great Recession is also different between GDP and FGDP using the three-quarter moving average (Table 5.3).

Figure 5.3 shows indices of GDP and FGDP (in 2009 prices) with base year 1987. Up to the end of 1990, the difference between changes in the two indicators[2] is around 1 percent. From 1991 to 1996 the two measures increasingly diverge, first by 3 percent and up to 6 percent in 1996. They then move closer together in 1997–1999, only to diverge more strongly from 2000 on, with an average difference of 11 percent since 2005.

Table 5.1 The 1990–1991 recession is deeper according to FGDP

	GDP	*FGDP*
1990Q4	−0.9%	−0.9%
1991Q1	−0.5%	−1.6%
Total	**−1.4%**	**−2.5%**

Table 5.2 The Great Recession is greater according to FGDP

	GDP	*FGDP*
2008Q4	−2.2%	−1.8%
2009Q1	−1.4%	−4.0%
2009Q2	−0.1%	−1.6%
Total	**−3.7%**	**−7.4%**

Table 5.3 The Great Recession is longer according to GDP, but deeper according to FGDP

	GDP	*FGDP*
2008Q2	−0.2%	0.1%
2008Q3	−0.7%	0.1%
2008Q4	−1.3%	−1.9%
2009Q1	−1.2%	−2.5%
2009Q2	−0.4%	−1.8%
Total	**−3.9%**	**−6.2%**

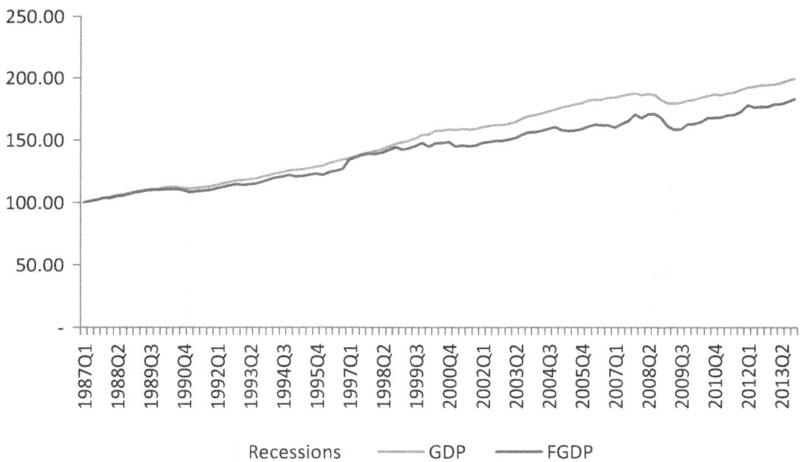

Figure 5.3 Indices of GDP and FGDP, 1987 = 100 with NBER recessions shaded

The data show a negative correlation (−0.3) between the extent of divergence of the two indicators (as measured by the difference between their rates of change) and the growth rate of GDP. Furthermore, regressing the difference between GDP and FGDP on the rate of growth of GDP (simple OLS with HAC standard errors) yields a regression coefficient of −2, significant at the 1 percent level (see Table 5.4). In other words, the higher the growth rate of GDP, the less it diverges from FGDP. This may be interpreted to mean that, if we accept FGDP as our benchmark, GDP is biased towards underestimating periods of slower or negative growth (stagnations and recessions). Regressing the difference on FGDP growth, meanwhile, has a smaller coefficient of −0.73, statistically significant at the 5 percent level, representing a smaller bias than that of GDP.

Table 5.4 Regression of difference between GDP and FGDP on GDP growth
OLS, using observations 1987:2–2013:4 (T = 107)
Dependent variable: difference, HAC standard errors, bandwidth 3 (Bartlett kernel)

	Coefficient	*Std. error*	*t-ratio*	*p-value*	
constant	0.078002	0.00884348	8.8203	<0.00001	***
GDP_Growth	−2.04542	0.71565	−2.8581	0.00514	***

Mean dependent var	0.064727	S.D. dependent var	0.042862
Sum squared resid	0.177692	S.E. of regression	0.041138
R-squared	0.087516	Adjusted R-squared	0.078826
F(1, 105)	8.168882	P-value(F)	0.005140
Log-likelihood	190.6022	Akaike criterion	−377.2044
Schwarz criterion	−371.8587	Hannan-Quinn	−375.0373
rho	0.912690	Durbin-Watson	0.160242

FGDP also crosses into negative territory more often, at least for single quarters. Looking beyond two quarters of negative growth – i.e. recessions according to the NBER definition – the quarterly growth data tell a much richer tale. From 1987 to 1994, differences between GDP and FGDP are the exception rather than the rule, occurring only four times in thirty-three quarters (that is, with a 12.1 percent incidence). From 1995 to 2004, differences occur regularly, with the incidence doubling to 25 percent. Starting in the second quarter of 2005, the two indices diverge so often that periods where they are identical are now the exception – only three quarters out of thirty-six (a divergence rate of 91.7 percent, or a coincidence rate of 8.3 percent only). This implies that FGDP becomes far more illuminating from the mid-1990s as a leading indicator. Sometimes it is ahead by a positive change, e.g. 1997Q1, 2002Q1, 2003Q1, and 2006Q1–Q2, 2007Q2–Q4, 2010Q3, 2011Q4–2012Q1, 2013Q1, and 2013Q4 – instances of charting a recovery earlier and faster than GDP. In other cases, FGDP is ahead in the tracking of stagnation and recession as mentioned above, turning negative already in 2006Q3, with GDP catching up only six quarters later in 2008Q1, *after* the financial crisis had already begun.

The analysis above examined the divergence of GDP and FGDP since 1995. Our thesis is that this is at least partly due to the fact that GDP's treatment of financial services as part of output is covering up stagnating or weakening demand. As dos Santos (2009) points out, "[l]ending to individuals has become a major part of banks' overall lending" (11), a claim supported by the data (93 percent of financial value added in 2012 was assigned to household consumption in the input–output tables). As opposed to financial services to enterprises, "[m]oney loaned out to individuals for consumption or mortgages does not ordinarily generate the value from which it is to be repaid with interest activities" (ibid.). We have seen in the previous chapter that fee-based financial revenues (value added) provided to firms are netted out of total value added as intermediate consumption, whereas services provided to households are counted as final consumption expenditure.

The national accounts thus ascribe a demand-stimulating role to financial services paid for by households, whereas in fact they can be more accurately thought of as a leakage out of aggregate demand. Similar to taxes, financial fees paid by individuals are not acts of consumption (since, as we argued in the previous chapter, credit and money have only an intermediate, not a final use, value), nor of production (by definition since households are consumers). They somewhat resemble savings in that they leave the circular flow of demand, but savings are at least owned by the depositor and can be used for future consumption or investment. Financial fees are lost forever to the paying party, as are taxes collected by governments.[3] Treating financial fees as taxes (one source of demand leakage) is also the demand-side equivalent of our theory of finance as an intermediate input on the supply (output) side, presented in the previous chapter.

Therefore, FGDP could be performing better than GDP as a leading indicator of secular stagnation precisely because it deducts financial fees as overall economic costs, treating them as leakages out of aggregate demand, while GDP shows these fees – increasingly associated with the creation of consumer debt – as final consumption expenditure. In other words, GDP may be suffering from a statistical bubble by treating demand-weakening (not to mention unsustainable) credit- and debt-related income as if it were adding to the demand for goods and services.

5.5 Forecasting with FGDP vs. GDP

Another way to evaluate GDP vs. FGDP as leading indicators is to conduct an out-of-sample forecast of changes in employment (as a proxy for aggregate demand) using part of the observations of GDP and FGDP. Based on the above reported divergence starting in 1995 between the two indicators, the sample was restricted to 1987–1994, and a forecast for 1995–2012 was conducted on the basis of an AR(1) model. Figure 5.4 shows the results of the forecast for each measure.

As a comparison of the two charts in Figure 5.4 illustrates, GDP completely missed the drop in demand and employment in the early

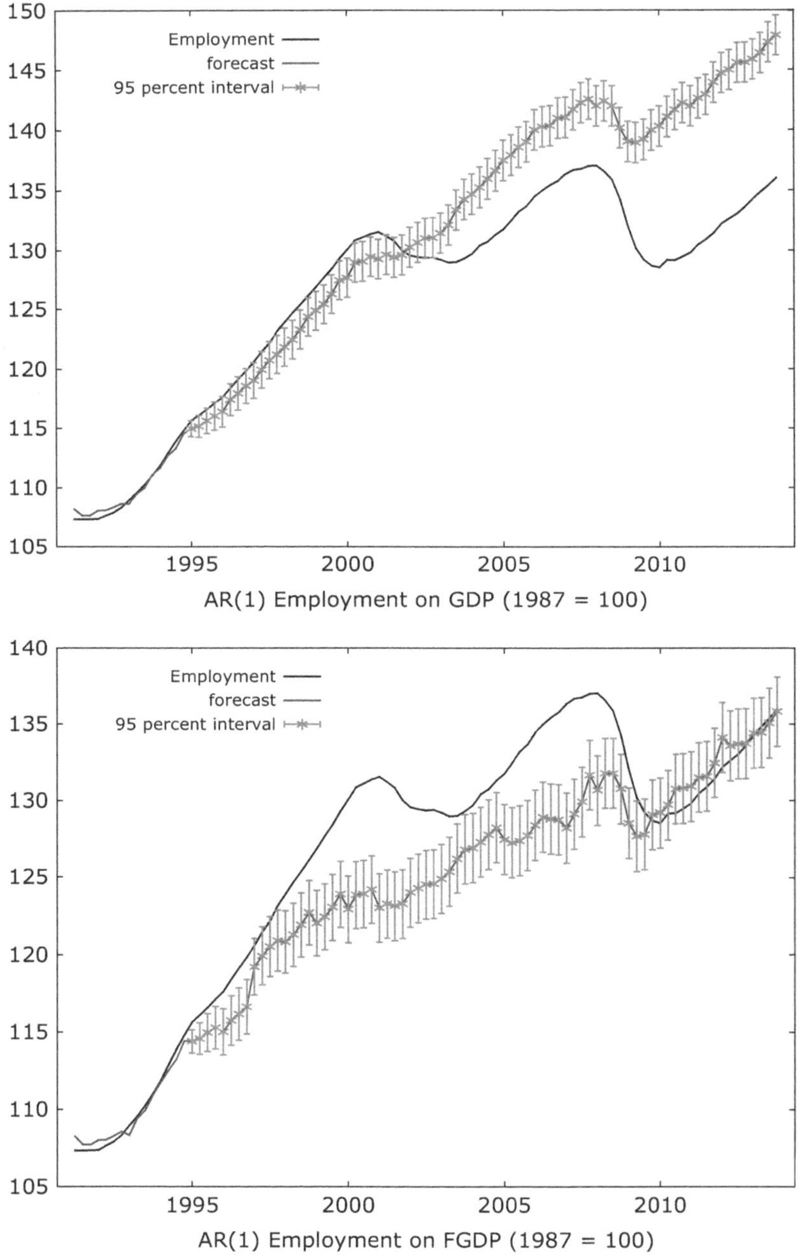

Figure 5.4 Forecasts of employment based on ARMAX, using quarterly observations 1987–1994

Table 5.5 Evaluation statistics for GDP and FGDP forecasts of employment, 1995–2012

	Mean error	*Mean squared error*	*Root mean squared error*	*Mean absolute error*	*Mean percentage error*	*Mean absolute percentage error*	*Theil's U*	*Bias proportion, UM*	*Regression proportion, UR*	*Disturbance proportion, UD*
GDP	−4.11	45.00	6.71	5.29	−3.08	4.03	9.84	0.38	0.48	0.15
FGDP	3.33	19.99	4.36	3.65	2.56	2.80	6.41	0.59	0.03	0.39

2000s, while FGDP showed the downturn as well as the recovery ahead of employment itself. As for the Great Recession, FGDP has been more pessimistic than employment would have suggested, finally converging with the latter at the depth of the crisis. GDP, meanwhile, has been happily overshooting employment since as early as 2000.

Table 5.5 provides overall forecast evaluation statistics for the entire period 1995–2012.

In addition to the fact that FGDP suffers from a smaller MSE and RMSE than GDP, it is interesting to note that it errs on the side of caution – its mean error is positive in both absolute and percentage terms (shown in Table 5.5's first and fifth columns respectively), while that of GDP is negative. In other words, FGDP's trend is closer to that of employment than GDP, but from below rather than above, foreshadowing, as it were, an overall trend of secular stagnation. One could therefore think that GDP and FGDP are specialized predictors of employment trends, the former performing better in "fair weather" (the Roaring 90s) and the latter in "foul weather" (the Great Recession and beyond). This conclusion, however, may be biased because of the relatively small sample used above (showing GDP as closer to the pre-2000 employment trends, and FGDP closer to the post-2000 trends).

Looking at annual data enables us to use a longer time series, and thus a better sample to forecast with. The OECD has data on value added since 1970. This was used once more in an out-of-sample forecast based on observations from 1970 to 1994, as shown in Figure 5.5.

The forecast based on the longer, annual time series is within the 95 percent confidence interval for FGDP, but still very much overshooting employment for GDP. Beyond the visual proximity, Table 5.6 provides overall forecast evaluation statistics for the entire period 1995–2012 based on the longer, annual time series 1970–1994.

FGDP's evaluation statistics based on the annual data forecast are quite similar to those based on its quarterly forecast. For GDP, however, the annual forecast based on the longer sample performs much worse, with an MSE almost four times as large and an RMSE twice as large as the quarterly forecast. Thus, an analyst using annual data to predict the trend of employment based on GDP would be quite misled. As the various indicators of forecast evaluation suggest, FGDP consistently performs better than GDP as a leading indicator for employment and thus of aggregate demand.

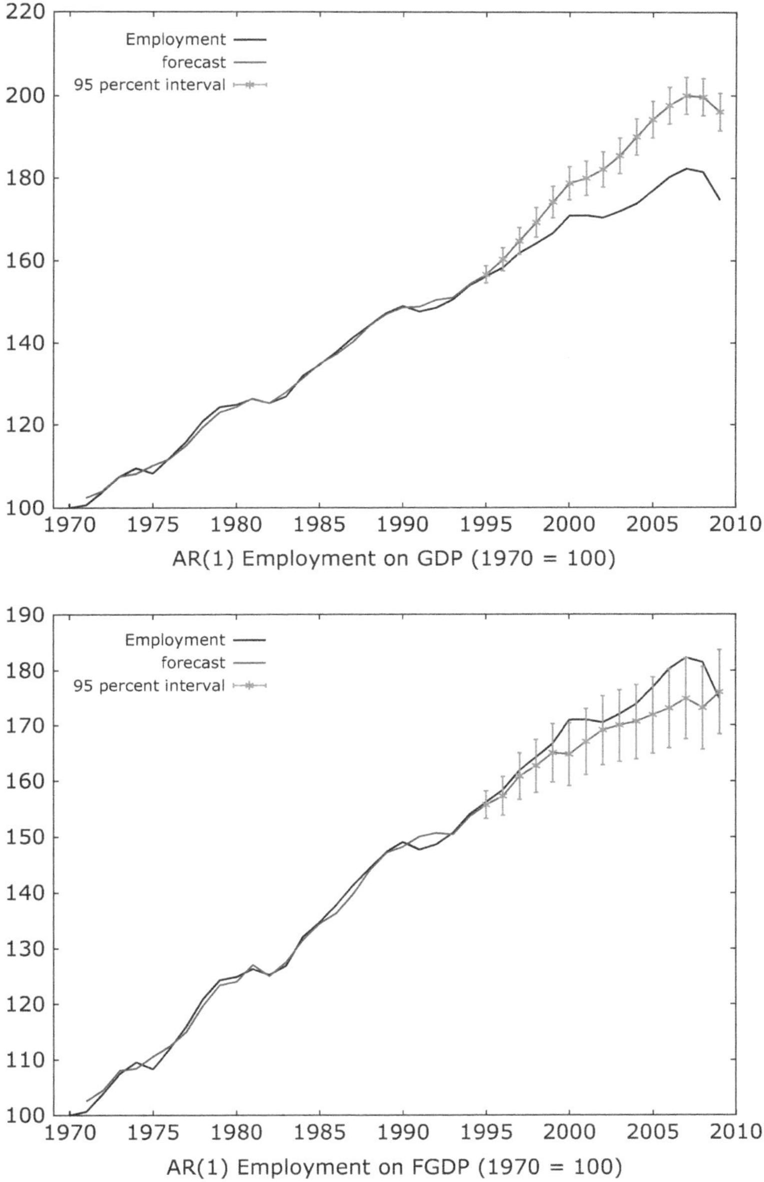

Figure 5.5 Forecasts of employment based on ARMAX, using annual observations 1970–1994

Table 5.6 Evaluation statistics for GDP and FGDP forecasts of employment, 1995–2012 based on the longer, annual time series 1970–1994

	Mean error	*Mean squared error*	*Root mean squared error*	*Mean absolute error*	*Mean percentage error*	*Mean absolute percentage error*	*Theil's U*	*Bias proportion, UM*	*Regression proportion, UR*	*Disturbance proportion, UD*
GDP	−11.17	167.00	12.92	11.17	−6.39	6.39	4.41	0.75	0.24	0.01
FGDP	3.31	18.96	4.35	3.48	1.89	1.98	1.49	0.58	0.09	0.33

5.6 Aggregate demand, output, and employment

The three leakages from aggregate demand are savings, taxes, and imports. Assuming that the marginal propensity to save and foreigners' demand are both unaffected by our new measure, taxes become the interesting part of the analysis. As argued above, financial fees are similar to taxes levied by government, in that they are taken out of the purchasing power available for final consumption of goods and services.

This has a direct effect on the multiplier. Recall that the multiplier with taxes is denoted as the first term on the right of the following expression:

$$Y = \frac{1}{(1-b+bt)}(a+I+G) \tag{1}$$

where Y is total income, b is the marginal propensity to consume, t is the tax rate, a is autonomous consumption, I is real private investment, and G is government expenditure. If we accept that financial fees levied on households are a form of tax, we can write:

$$Y = \frac{1}{(1-b+bt+bf)}(a+I+G) \tag{2}$$

with f as the rate of financial levy and all other variables unchanged. As long as f is positive – that is, financial charges are a positive proportion of disposable income – the denominator will be larger, resulting in a smaller multiplier, and thus a smaller response of aggregate demand and output to any initial change in autonomous demand.

To examine the demand sensitivity of GDP and FGDP vis-à-vis employment, we build on the following framework: the spending that is the outcome of increased demand leads, in turn, to increased output and thus higher employment. We construct indices for standard GDP, employment, non-financial GDP or NFGDP (based on Basu and Foley's NFVA adjusted for taxes less subsidies) and narrow-measured GDP or NMGDP (Basu and Foley's NMVA adjusted likewise), and our measure of FGDP. We expect FGDP to be more closely correlated with employment than GDP, NFGDP or NMGDP, since (1) finance does not contribute to total output (having no final use-value but only an intermediate role as a cost of production), and (2) finance has a negative correlation between output and employment shares, as shown in the previous chapter. Other service sectors excluded from NMGDP (such education, health, etc.), however, do have final use, and, as argued above, must involve production and employment.

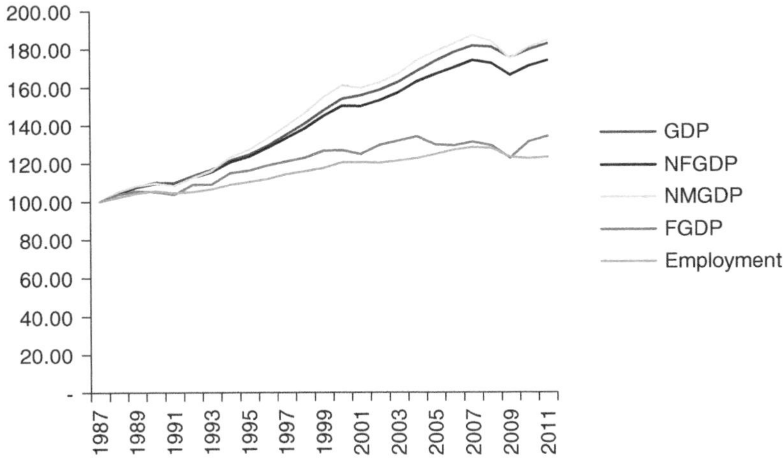

Figure 5.6 Indices of GDP, non-financial GDP, narrow-measured GDP, final GDP, and employment, 1987–2011

Using real growth rates (with an index based on 1987 = 100), Figure 5.6 shows that the FGDP index most closely tracks employment over the period 1987–2011. In this analysis the NMGDP measure is more closely related to official GDP than was the NMVA index in Basu and Foley's original paper. This is due to the fact that GDP differs from value added by including taxes net of subsidies.

Beyond the visual proximity of FGDP and employment, how can we assess whether it is a "better fit" for our purposes than GDP? As we are interested in the relationship between output and employment, we regress the employment index (based on Bureau of Labor Statistics data) on each of the four output indices shown in Figure 5.6, with the results shown in Table 5.7.

All regression coefficients are statistically significant at the 1 percent level, but FGDP has a far better fit with the independent variable – employment – than the other three measures. FGDP can thus help explain the otherwise mysterious phenomena of jobless recoveries and job-loss downturns mentioned by Basu and Foley, where employment moves much more slowly than what changes in standard GDP would imply. Using FGDP, the "jobless" recoveries appear as periods of stagnation, where job creation is naturally minimal, resolving the apparent mystery.

Using OECD data enables us to go back as far as 1970. This view confirms the conclusions drawn above, as can be seen in Figure 5.7. The regression coefficients are even more pronounced with the longer time series, with 0.36 for GDP, 0.49 for NFGDP, and 0.79 for FGDP.

As Figure 5.8 further illustrates, GDP shows the US economy growing around 4 percent from 1992 to 2000, while FGDP and employment grew at an average of 2.3 percent and 1.6 percent, respectively. Likewise, 2001 had an annual growth of 1.1 percent for GDP, but −1.6 percent for FGDP and zero employment growth. Furthermore, the recovery from the 2001 recession was a healthy 2.7 percent average over 2002–2006 according to GDP, but a more synchronized 0.7 percent in FGDP and 1.1 percent in employment.

Table 5.7 Regression coefficients. OLS, using observations 1987–2011 (T = 25), dependent variable: employment HAC standard errors, bandwidth 2 (Bartlett kernel)

	Coefficient
GDP	0.301547
NFGDP	0.339159
NMGDP	0.288879
FGDP	0.760439

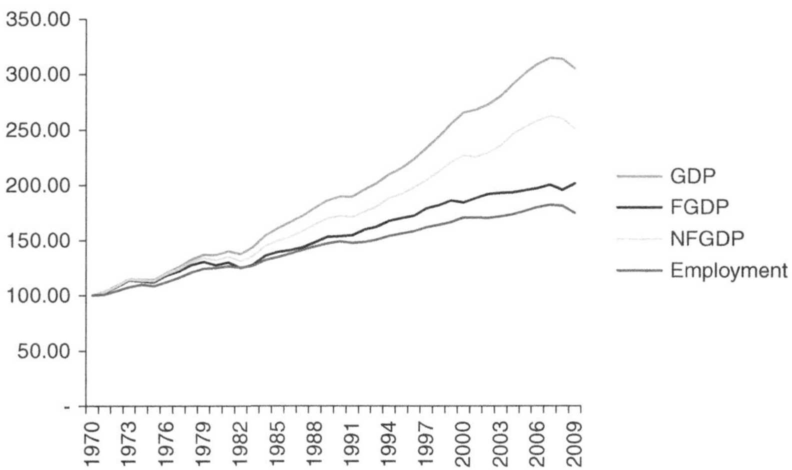

Figure 5.7 Indices of GDP, non-financial GDP, narrow-measured GDP, usable GDP, and employment, 1970–2009

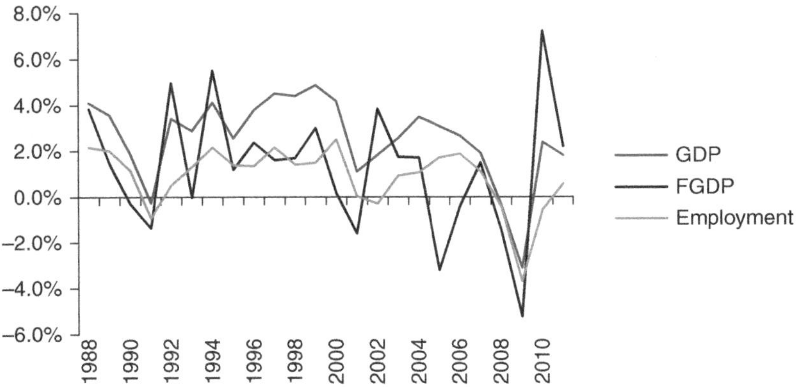

Figure 5.8 Changes in GDP, FGDP and employment 1987–2011

5.7 Okun's revenge: output and unemployment fluctuations

Another spurious puzzle that can be explained by FGDP is the breakdown of Okun's Law. Arthur Okun's finding in 1962 of a negative relationship between output and unemployment in the short run has been confirmed by many subsequent empirical findings and has featured regularly in textbooks. A consensus estimate for the US is that a 1 percent fall in output causes a rise of half a point in the unemployment rate (Ball *et al.*, 2013, BLL below). In recent literature, however, many have questioned the continued relevance of this law, either because of structural changes (Gordon, 2010), its instability in some countries (Cazes *et al.*, 2012, Knotek, 2007), the "jobless recoveries" following the last three recessions in the US, or a breakdown of the law during the Great Recession (IMF, 2010). BLL, meanwhile, reaffirm the strength and stability of Okun's Law using data from 1948 for the US (and from 1980 for twenty advanced economies), though they find substantive variation in the coefficient relating changes in output and unemployment across countries (due mostly to idiosyncratic labor market features).

What can our alternative measure, FGDP, add to this debate? The various parties to this macroeconomic dispute focus on whether or not there was a structural break in the economy in the mid-1980s or early 1990s (similar to the discussion about the Great Moderation above). Both sides use GDP as their preferred measure of output. There is, therefore, a possibility that the proper measurement of output is part of the issue. Basu and Foley (2013) point in this direction, observing that the growth in services "systematically leads to real GDP overestimating real output at the aggregate level, which explains part of the apparent breakdown of Okun's Law" (1100).

As Gordon (2010) observes, the last three recessions have been followed by "jobless recoveries," which is offered as proof for the breakdown of Okun's Law. As we argued above, however, jobless recoveries are not real, since FGDP shows them as periods of stagnation, and we have seen that FGDP tracks employment trends better than GDP. This would imply that, rather than Okun's Law breaking down recently, it is measurement of aggregate activity that has broken down as GDP has become financialized (especially since the 1993 SNA "made" finance productive). Similar to the spurious debate about the Great Moderation, replacing GDP with FGDP solves the problem and shows that yet another contemporary macro debate has more to do with measurement issues than anything more fundamental about the workings of the economy.

The original formulation by Okun related the unemployment rate to the output gap (potential output less actual output):

$$U_t = \beta\,(Y_t - Y_t^*) + \varepsilon_t \qquad (1)$$

Since Y* is unobservable, however, we estimate the "changes" version of the Law (BLL, 5):

$$\Delta U_t = \alpha + \beta\,\Delta Y_t + \omega_t \qquad (2)$$

Table 5.8 presents the results of regressing percentage-point changes in the unemployment rate on percentage changes in output, as measured by GDP and FGDP respectively. The regression was performed first for the full period (1970–2012) and for the second period (1986–2006), which, according to Gordon, saw the breakdown of Okun's Law.

The results of the two regressions show that, for the whole period 1970–2012, FGDP is closer to Okun's original prediction of 0.33 for

Table 5.8 Regression coefficients, OLS, dependent variable: ΔU

	Coefficient	*p-value*	R^2
1970–2012 (T = 43)			
GDP	−0.20	0.00	0.79
FGDP	−0.44	0.00	0.87
1986–2012 (T = 21)			
GDP	−0.08	0.00	0.59
FGDP	−0.23	0.00	0.80

the coefficient relating output changes to changes in the unemployment rate. More importantly, the second part of the table shows that the GDP coefficient is far lower in the later period, whereas FGDP is still meaningful. Furthermore, the R^2 of the GDP coefficient drops from 0.79 for the whole period to only 0.59 for the later period, indicating that changes in GDP explain less of the variation in the rate of unemployment than they did before 1986, and less than changes in FGDP explain throughout the period. Overall, then, while there is a reduction in the Okun coefficient using both GDP and FGDP, the former presents the period 1986–2012 as a virtual breakdown of Okun's Law (since a −0.08 coefficient means it would take a 12.5 percent drop in output to raise the unemployment rate by one percentage point), whereas FGDP still shows the relevance of Okun's observation, although with a slightly lower coefficient (roughly a 4 percent drop in output in 1986–2012 is required to raise the unemployment rate by one percentage point, compared with 3 percent for the longer period 1970–2012).

5.8 Aggregate demand and the velocity of money

Another side of the same coin can be seen in the relationship between aggregate demand and the speed of transactions in an economy. In a demand-based framework, it is possible to test the relevance of FGDP for measuring aggregate demand using the equation of exchange, $M * V = P * Q$, where M is the quantity of money in circulation, V is the transactions velocity of money, P is an index of the price level, and Q is a measure of real output. While neoclassical (monetarist) thinking posits that changes in the supply of money affect only prices, Keynesian theory considers the possibility of changes in M affecting Q as well. Either way, the reason for using this equation here is that the velocity of money can be a proxy for consumption demand – an increase in the velocity of money implying rising demand, and vice versa. As the Federal Reserve Bank of St. Louis explains in the notes to its data, "[t]he frequency of currency exchange can be used to determine the velocity of a given component of the money supply, providing some insight into whether consumers and businesses are saving or spending their money" (Federal Reserve Bank of St. Louis, 2014).

The Federal Reserve tracks the velocity of three components of money supply:[4]

- M1 is the narrowest component, including currency in circulation as well as demand and checkable deposits. If the velocity of M1 is decreasing, this could indicate a drop in short-term (i.e. everyday) consumption.

- M2 is broader than M1 and includes, additionally, saving deposits, certificates of deposit (less than $100,000). and individual money market deposits. Comparing M1 and M2 velocities gives some insight into the speed of spending and saving in the economy.
- Finally, MZM is money with zero maturity, the broadest component of the money supply. It includes "the supply of financial assets redeemable at par on demand: notes and coins in circulation, traveler's checks (non-bank issuers), demand deposits, other checkable deposits, savings deposits, and *all* money market funds. The velocity of MZM helps determine how often financial assets are switching hands within the economy" (ibid., emphasis added).

The velocity of the money stock is calculated as the ratio of nominal GDP to the average of the money stock (Federal Reserve Bank of St. Louis, 2014), i.e. V = Q*P/M. If we use FGDP instead of GDP for Q, holding M and P constant, what would be the effect on V and, by implication, on aggregate demand? To test the effect of using FGDP instead of GDP on the derived measure of the velocity of money (as a proxy for aggregate demand), two indices were constructed and rebased to 1987 (the first year for which data are available for calculating FGDP). V^ represents the derived velocity of money using standard GDP and M1, and F^ represents the same ratio for FGDP and M1. As a decreasing velocity of money "might indicate fewer consumption transactions taking place" (ibid.), the use of FGDP suggests a lower and faster-decreasing level of demand in the US economy, with the decrease accelerating from 1996 onwards – see Figure 5.9.

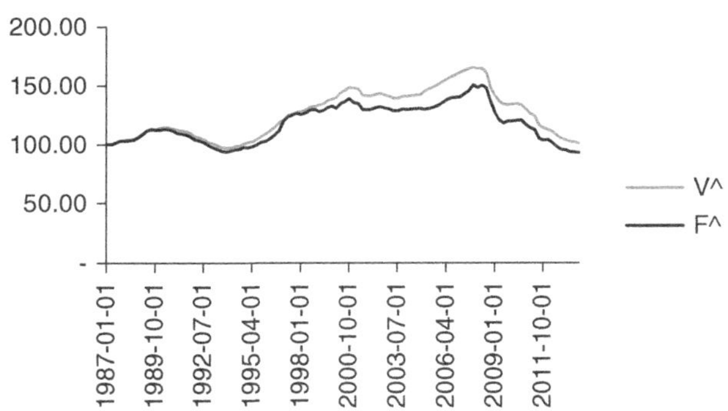

Figure 5.9 Indices of quarterly velocity of money (M1) calculated using GDP and FGDP

Both series in Figure 5.9 show a dip in the early 1990s followed by a rise, but then start to diverge (mirroring the divergence of GDP and FGDP since 1995 discussed above). While the excess of V^ over F^ was 3 percent until 1994, this difference began accelerating in the buildup to the 2007 recession, reaching double digits in 2005–2006 (with V^ on average 13 percent higher than F^). Both indices show that the decline in short-term consumption had not yet been reversed as of 2012.

Figure 5.10 plots a similar comparison of velocities for M2. As mentioned above, M2 velocities indicate how quickly spending (and saving) occurs in the economy.

Here the difference in implied demand between GDP and FGDP is starker. While both series suggest a secular stagnation or even a lower trend in the level of aggregate demand after 1995 (once again the point of divergence), V^ – based on GDP – appears to have a statistical bubble, rising 5.9 percent from 2003Q2 to 2006Q2, and only starting its decline then; F^ rises only 2.1 percent over the same period, thus showing FGDP as leading GDP by twelve quarters (three years). Given that the early 2000s saw growing financial and real-estate bubbles, F^ presents a more somber, though plausible, view of the US economy as never quite recovering from the dot.com recession. Additionally, V^ portrays the trough of 2009–2011 as having the same speed of spending as 1987, while F^ suggests that spending had declined to 90 percent of that level at the bottom of the crisis.

Finally, looking at the velocity of the broadest monetary aggregate – MZM – the two indices are more in line with each other than in the case of M2. From 2004Q2 to 2006Q2, V^ increases by 7.4 percent compared

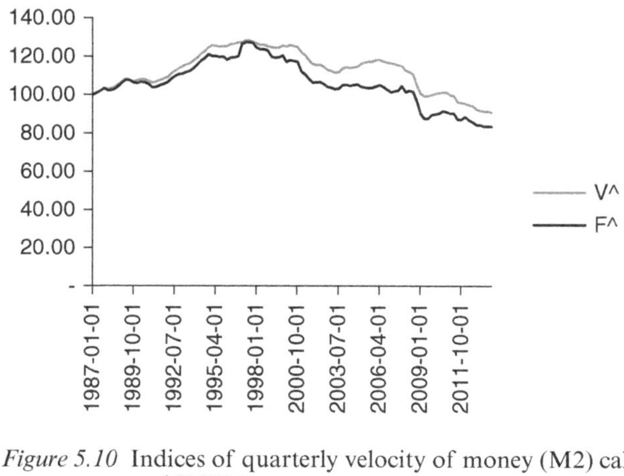

Figure 5.10 Indices of quarterly velocity of money (M2) calculated using GDP and FGDP

with 4.0 percent in F^. This is to be expected since MZM measures the speed of circulation of financial assets rather than spending on goods and services (M2) or short-term consumption (M1). If GDP is a financialized indicator, as we argued above, it performs well for capturing this part of transactions in the economy. For the purposes of estimating overall aggregate demand for goods and services, however, M2 is a more appropriate measure of velocity than MZM, and hence FGDP is a better fit for this purpose.

F^2 (the velocity of M2 based on FGDP) may be interpreted as too cautious (or pessimistic) an indicator, given that it mostly shows negative changes during the period 1996–2009 (Figure 5.10). If the decreases in the velocity of money signal drops in consumption as suggested above, however, in a demand-driven economy F^2 would thus be a better leading indicator signaling recessions a year or two earlier than the Fed's M2V, which is based on standard GDP. The most extreme example is the buildup to the 2007 crises. V^2 in Figure 5.11 shows a drop in demand below the 2001 level only in 2007, whereas F^2 shows that demand has never fully recovered from the 2001 recession (which also looks deeper using the latter measure than using the former). Put another way, during the 2000s FGDP (and the F^2 measure derived from it) clearly signals a hidden tendency towards secular stagnation. The reason this trend is hidden is that, while aggregate demand had indeed increased during the 2000s, this increase was due only to increased borrowing leading to an increased endogenous creation of money (to the extent the increases in bank credit met at least some part of the increased borrowing).

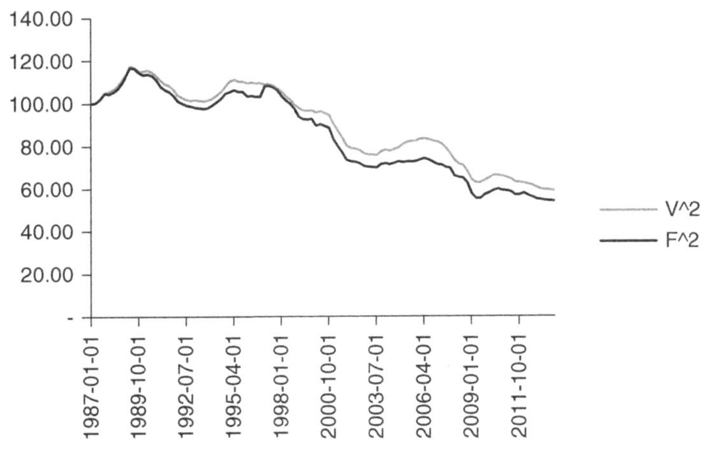

Figure 5.11 Indices of quarterly velocity of money (MZM) calculated using GDP and FGDP

From a monetarist point of view, these findings do not condone the use of FGDP as it presents the velocity of money as less stable than does GDP, since monetarists consider the velocity to be independent of the quantity of money. Thus Fisher writes, "The average rate of turnover...will depend on the density of population, commercial customs, rapidity of transport and other technical conditions, but not on the quantity of money" (1911, 155). Keynes, by contrast, thought that money velocity depends on "many complex and variable factors," so assuming a constant velocity of money would disguise "the real character of causation" (1936, 299). These variable factors include liquidity preference and various interest elasticities of expenditure (Higgins, 1978). The picture is further complicated, as we have now seen, by the choice of output measure used to compute the velocity, as well as the fact that much of the circulation of money occurs in transactions that do not create value added (such as finance, insurance, and real estate, as argued in this essay).

Notes

1 'Deterioration' implies that GDP had once been a better indicator of aggregate demand. Whether this is true is open to argument, but is beyond the scope of this work. As mentioned in the previous chapter, however, Christophers (2011) provides an excellent summary of how financial intermediation moved across the production boundary in the national accounts, comprising a deterioration of sorts if one accepts our thesis that finance is a cost, or at least the intermediate view that it is not a productive sector.

2 Calculated as the index ratio (GDP/FGDP − 1)*100.

3 While governments provide services with final use-value – education, health, public administration, and security – our argument would suggest that financial services merely trade in credit, or exchange value. Either way, however, the analogy between fee-based financial services and government taxes is useful since the funds are taken out of the circular flow of aggregate demand.

4 M3 is no longer tracked by the Federal Reserve.

6 The distributional impacts of FGDP

6.1 The changing structure of demand by expenditure categories

The appendix to Chapter 4 demonstrated how, in order to reconcile the output-based FGDP aggregate to the income and expenditure approaches of national accounting, we must use the more detailed input–output tables. As the quote from Leontief at the beginning of the previous chapter suggests, this rich data source will also be necessary to evaluate the distributional impacts of using FGDP.

Starting on the expenditure side, Figures 6.1 and 6.2 show the different distribution of expenditure categories using GDP vs. FGDP. These are final consumption expenditure (FCE), gross fixed capital

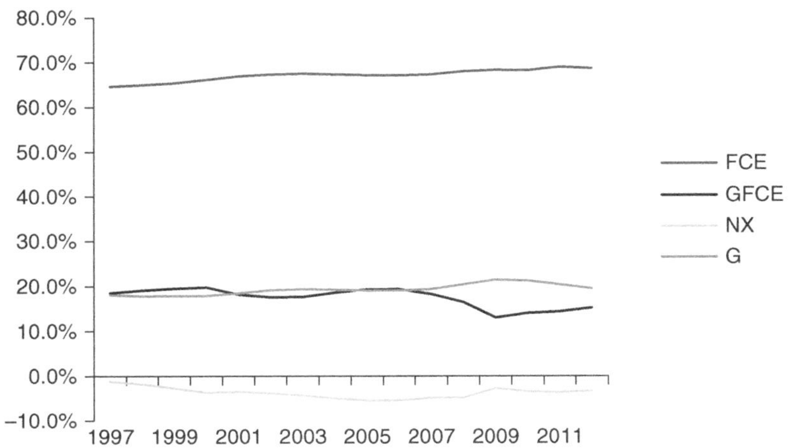

Figure 6.1 Distribution of GDP by expenditure, % of total
Source: author's calculations from NIPA input–output tables for 1997–2012 (individual years)

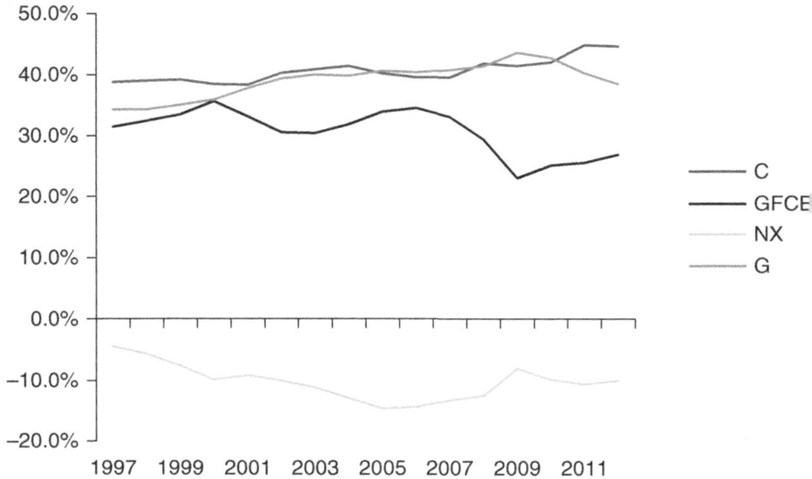

Figure 6.2 Distribution of FGDP by expenditure, % of total

Source: author's calculations from NIPA input–output tables for 1997–2012 (individual years)

expenditure (GFCE, or investment), net exports (NX) and government expenditure (G).

The figures show several important implications of FGDP for the distribution of expenditures in the US economy. First, in terms of the movement of shares over time, FGDP presents a more volatile picture (as it did in the aggregate in Chapter 5), especially in regards to investment spending (GFCE). Investment and the balance of trade deteriorate much more dramatically starting in 2006 and 2003, respectively, when viewed through the lens of FGDP. The mean standard deviation of each category is shown in Table 6.1.

Second, final consumption expenditure is no longer the largest category of spending. Whereas GDP shows it to be three times as large as government spending, FGDP shows these two expenditure categories as roughly equal. Investment, while dropping by half in absolute terms, is now relatively larger than before, averaging 30.6 percent of FGDP compared with 17.4 percent of GDP. This is due to the biggest absolute reduction occurring in final consumption (which in GDP accounts for 93.4 percent of financial total income or value added), while only 3.2 percent of investment spending was on finance according to GDP (remember that most fees charged to firms are netted out as intermediate

Table 6.1 Mean standard deviation of expenditure shares in GDP and FGDP, 1997–2012

	Mean standard deviation	
Expenditure category	*GDP*	*FGDP*
FCE	1.3%	2.0%
GFCE	2.1%	3.7%
NX	1.2%	2.9%
G	1.1%	2.9%

consumption and do not show up as part of output). Investment also has more pronounced peaks and troughs under FGDP in both the dot. com boom and the Great Recession. Net exports are also lower, averaging −10.2 percent of FGDP instead of −3.8 percent of GDP. Their share of financial value added was small – 3.4 percent – hence the magnitude of the change. The direction of the change in net exports' relative share of expenditure implies that the US was exporting more financial services than it was importing, so taking out finance would show up as deterioration in its balance of trade.

Third, and most importantly, this difference in relative importance of expenditure shares has a critical implication for the structure of aggregate demand. Government spending and investment – two of the three autonomous expenditure injections to demand – are now more important than when viewed through the lens of GDP, whereas consumption – not exclusively autonomous since it depends on income through the marginal propensity to consume – is no longer the undisputed driver of the economy, but rather *primus inter pares*. The political economy significance of this statistical coup d'état cannot be overstated: far more now depends on autonomous spending in the form of fiscal policy as well as real investment than on a passive dependence on a supposedly powerful consumer (whose disposable income, by the way, is also lower under FGDP, as will be shown below).

6.2 Implications for distribution by income

Moving on to the income side, Figures 6.3 and 6.4 show the different distribution of income categories using GDP vs. FGDP.

To get a more precise idea of the changes this makes to the level and trend of factor distribution, Table 6.2 shows both wage and profit shares for GDP and FGDP.

The two graphs in Figure 6.5 likewise compare the wage and profit shares of GDP and FGDP.

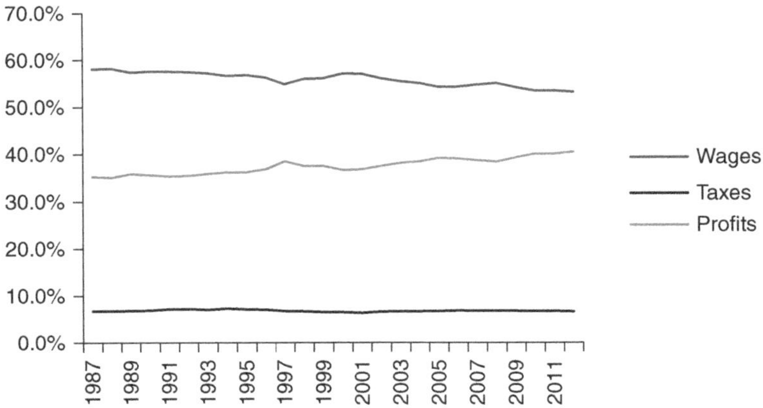

Figure 6.3 Distribution of GDP by income, % of total

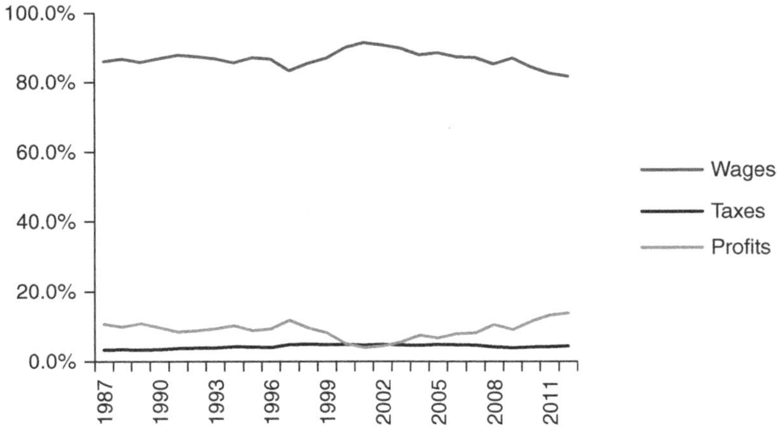

Figure 6.4 Distribution of FGDP by income, % of total

Similar to the comparison of GDP vs. FGDP on the expenditure side, the figures show two striking differences between the two measures. In terms of relative shares, labor income (including both wages and benefits) is even more important in FGDP than in GDP, averaging 86.8 percent of income in the former to 55.8 percent in the latter. As explained above, this is due to a larger share of deduction falling on the profit side, based on the profit-heavy income of the financial sector. The drop from

Table 6.2 Factor shares in GDP and FGDP, 1987–2012

	GDP	*FGDP*	*GDP*	*FGDP*
	Wages	*Wages*	*Profits*	*Profits*
1987	58.1%	86.1%	35.2%	10.7%
1988	58.2%	86.8%	35.1%	9.8%
1989	57.4%	85.8%	35.8%	10.9%
1990	57.6%	86.9%	35.6%	9.7%
1991	57.5%	87.9%	35.3%	8.4%
1992	57.4%	87.5%	35.4%	8.7%
1993	57.1%	86.8%	35.8%	9.3%
1994	56.6%	85.6%	36.2%	10.2%
1995	56.7%	87.1%	36.2%	8.8%
1996	56.2%	86.7%	36.8%	9.3%
1997	54.8%	83.4%	38.5%	11.8%
1998	55.9%	85.5%	37.4%	9.6%
1999	56.0%	87.0%	37.5%	8.2%
2000	57.0%	90.0%	36.6%	5.1%
2001	57.0%	91.4%	36.7%	3.9%
2002	56.0%	90.7%	37.4%	4.4%
2003	55.4%	89.8%	38.1%	5.5%
2004	55.0%	87.9%	38.4%	7.5%
2005	54.2%	88.5%	39.1%	6.7%
2006	54.2%	87.3%	39.0%	7.9%
2007	54.6%	87.2%	38.6%	8.2%
2008	55.0%	85.3%	38.3%	10.6%
2009	54.1%	87.0%	39.2%	9.1%
2010	53.3%	84.4%	40.0%	11.4%
2011	53.3%	82.6%	40.0%	13.2%
2012	53.1%	81.7%	40.4%	13.9%

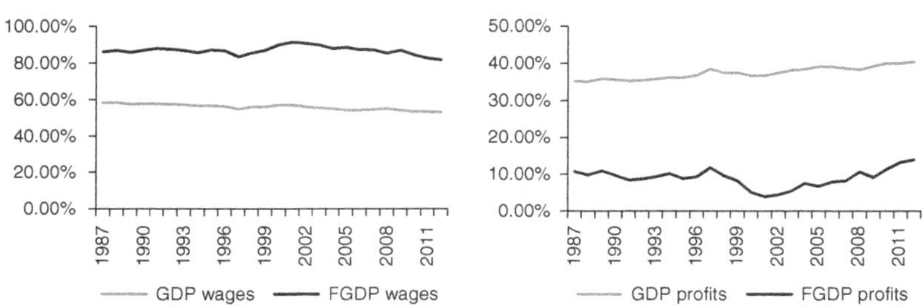

Figure 6.5 A comparison of the wage and profit shares of GDP and FGDP

Table 6.3 Mean standard deviation of income shares in GDP and FGDP, 1987–2012

	Mean standard deviation	
Income category	*GDP*	*FGDP*
Wages	1.5%	2.3%
Taxes	0.2%	0.5%
Profits	1.6%	2.5%

the 2001 peak wage share to the financial crisis in 2007, therefore, was 4.3 percent under GDP but 4.9 percent under FGDP (from 57.0 percent and 91.4 percent, respectively).

Second, both wage and profit shares are more volatile under FGDP, by roughly 50 percent (Table 6.3).

It seems that by including financial fees in its income or value added, GDP shows a smoother picture of economic trends, masking the volatility in the non-financial economy. This volatility extends beyond the profit and wage shares *per se*, and is even more dramatically evident if we chart the ratio of the two, i.e. the wage share divided by profit share. As Figure 6.6 illustrates, the proportion is flat for GDP, whereas in FGDP it peaks in 2001 (when the wage share at 91.4 percent was more than twenty-three times the profit share of 3.9 percent), and declines afterwards.

This is a curious finding, which on the surface is not very reassuring for our FGDP concept, since distribution is thought to be a fairly stable and slow-moving variable. Put in context, however, the variability of the wage/profit ratio in FGDP corresponds quite well with the series of household debt service payments – TDSP – from the St. Louis Fed, shown in Figure 6.7.

Since GDP includes payments made by households to financial firms as part of final expenditure, this transfer from labor to capital creates a smoothing effect in GDP that could mask more variability in profit and wage shares. To test this theory, we regressed both ratios (W/P GDP and W/P FGDP) on TDSP. The results are shown in Table 6.4.

There is a large, positive, and statistically significant relationship between the total debt service payments of households and the wage-to-profit share ratio in FGDP, but not in GDP.

What are the political economy implications of these findings? First, the difference between the relative shares of wages and profits in GDP vs. FGDP implies a different level of economic importance for labor

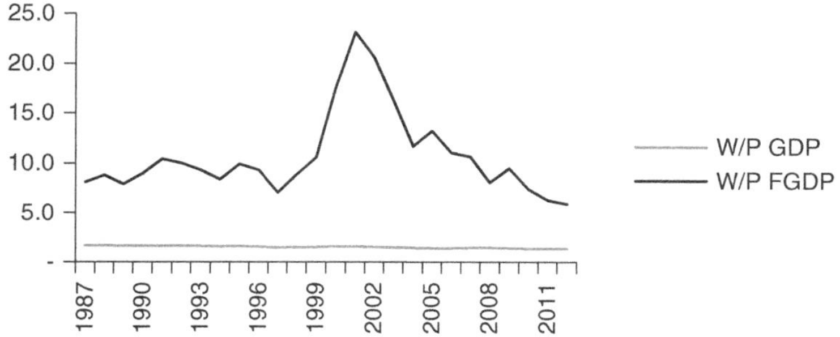

Figure 6.6 Proportion of the wage share to the profit share using GDP and FGDP

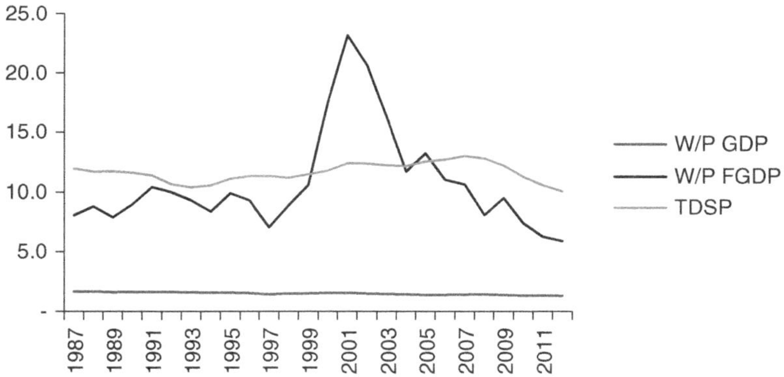

Figure 6.7 Ratios of wage share to the profit share using GDP and FGDP, and household debt service payments

Table 6.4 Regression coefficients. AR(1) regression, Cochrane-Orcutt, using observations 1988–2012 (T = 25) Explanatory variable: TDSP

	Coefficient	*p-value*	R^2
W/P GDP	0.02	0.43	0.86
W/P FGDP	2.67	0.02	0.71

and capital. Profit is earned by capitalist firms, which are often presented by politicians and lobbyists as job creators. But if profit counts for just 10–15 percent of GDP whereas labor income (wages plus benefits) counts for 80–85 percent, it is labor that is more responsible for the lion's share of economic activity (since much of what standard GDP reports as profits are merely transfers of financial fees). This ought to imply a policy shift, seeing tax cuts for households as more important than those for firms. In addition to household tax cuts, the importance of supporting the minimum wage, stable and dignified pensions, and low-cost health and education come to the forefront, since, to paraphrase Charles Erwin Wilson,[1] what's good for labor is good for the country (according to FGDP at any rate).

6.3 Implications for median and disposable income

Our discussion above portrayed financial fees as a leakage from aggregate demand akin to a tax, and emphasized their potential to retard demand at the macroeconomic level. At the microeconomic level, FGDP can help to more closely approximate a country's average standard of living in per capita form, since GDP per capita does not match people's experience very well (Stiglitz *et al.*, 2009). As Figure 6.8 shows, the average person's standard of living in terms of median income has stagnated since 1987, while standard GDP per capita shows a 47 percent improvement, peaking in 2007. FGDP, meanwhile, demonstrates only a 6 percent improvement in the same period, and has a trough in 2009 of 2.5 percent lower per capita FGDP than in 1987 (by contrast, in 2009 per capita GDP was 39.5 percent higher than in 1987).

This divergence of FGDP from GDP (and the closer proximity of the former to median income) suggests that, while financial corporations and wealthy investors did very well from the mid-1990s onwards, the rest of society – and the economy as a whole – did not.[2] Since our approach treats finance as a cost, the staggering growth in the size and income of the financial sector thus comes at the expense of the non-financial economy.

Pressman and Scott (2009) perform a similar analysis at the micro level by deducting interest payments on consumer debt from household income, and the results show a higher poverty rate in 2006 than standard figures would imply (including an additional 4 million debt-poor people in the US who do not count as poor otherwise). The logic is similar to the FGDP adjustment, but focusing on fees rather than interest differentials. Both income streams reduce the income effectively available for consumption, rendering disposable income (based on GDP) an inaccurate measure of actual purchasing power.

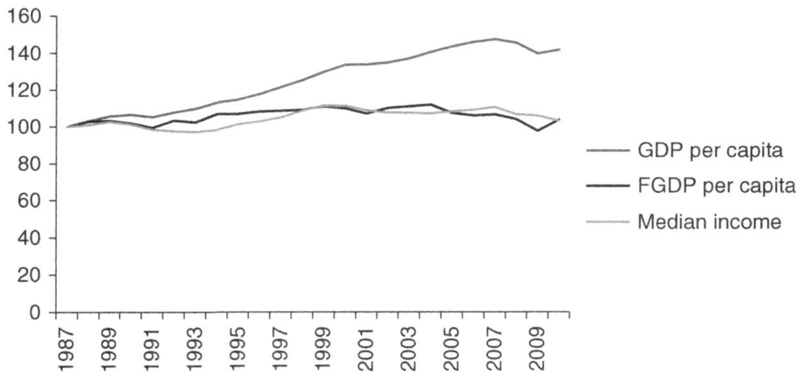

Figure 6.8 Indices of per capita GDP, per capita FGDP, and median household income, 1987–2010

Dos Santos (2009) documents the reorientation of bank lending away from firms and towards "direct extraction of revenues from ordinary wage-earners". Unlike lending by financial corporations to non-financial corporations – which tends to be a "mutually beneficial, arm's-length relationship" – the asymmetrical relationship between banks and individuals constitutes "historically new, *exploitative* modes of appropriation from the independently secured income of wage earners" (ibid., 3, emphasis in original). Workers' income is independent in the sense that the value appropriated from workers has been created without the help of a loan (unlike business loans). The asymmetry exists in terms of both the specialist nature of banks vs. the average worker (information asymmetry) and the forced nature of much individual borrowing, due to "[t]he privatization of provision for a number of basic social necessities," such as housing, education, and pensions (ibid., 13). Dos Santos documents the increase in household financial obligations (from 15.4 percent of disposable income in 1980 to 19.4 percent in 2007), which – seen in the light of our view of financial fees as a form of taxation – suggests another reason for the weakening of aggregate demand.[3] This could also be conceptualized as a financialization of exploitation, away from appropriation of surplus value from the individual qua wage earner and towards extraction of financial surplus value from the individual as consumer.

Notes

1 Former president of General Motors and United States Secretary of Defense from 1953 to 1957.

2 It also supports our critique of GDP in general, and its treatment of financial incomes in particular, highlighting what may be thought of as another statistical bubble.

3 A dramatic example of this leakage of demand from consumers (who generally have a high marginal propensity to consume) to financiers (who have a lower one) is given by dos Santos (2009), where 89.1% of gains from mutual funds investment (from 1980 to 2005) were appropriated as commissions and fees by fund managers and firms, leaving retail investors only a meager 10.9% of the equity gain in their portfolio (p. 19).

7 Conclusion

The last two chapters have argued that the standard measure of economic income and production – GDP – has become financialized in recent decades due to both its inclusion of asset-creating and trading activities (the FIRE sectors) and the increasing weight of these sectors in the income structure of the actual economy. As a result, GDP has suffered from three key weaknesses – poor performance as a leading indicator for booms and busts; weakening correlation with proxies of aggregate demand such as employment, the velocity of consumption transactions, and the relative importance of various spending categories in the overall demand structure; and a loss of relevance for purposes of representing the average standard of living.

We have argued that, viewing financial fees as taxes, we can better understand their role as leakages out of aggregate demand, and that an indicator that deducts them as such – FGDP – would improve on GDP in all three categories (as a leading indicator, proxy for aggregate demand, and measure of standard of living). FGDP indeed performs better than GDP on all three fronts, as the evidence provided above suggests. In addition to these economic and statistical advantages, however, FGDP implies several important political economy conclusions.

First, FGDP's income share structure reinforces the view that labor income – not capital's profits – drives economic activity and creates jobs, implying a bigger need to tailor tax, wage, and pension policies (in addition to reducing the cost of basic services) to strengthen this motor of the economy (individuals here considered qua workers, not consumers).

Second, using GDP to understand the economy is misleading precisely because the inclusion of financial services covers up stagnations and recessionary trends by creating statistical bubbles that rise with financial incomes rather than tracking demand, output, and employment.

Third, by looking at the different structure of expenditures visible through FGDP as well as the weakening of consumption and thus the multiplier due to the FIRE tax, it is clear that autonomous injections to demand, such as investment and government spending, are far more important than GDP portrays them to be. This opens the door to more radical deployments of public spending, as well as public and private investment (e.g. in infrastructure) to boost the economy's growth rate and resilience.

Fourth, seeing FIRE as a tax (leakage) makes regulation of these sectors more important. This is not just because their activities take away resources from production and trade of goods and services, but also because of the quasi-feudal structure of incomes in these industries. For example, one could argue that retail investors should get a larger share of equity gains than the meager 10 percent averaged between 1980 and 2005 (with the rest swallowed as fees and commissions by the financial *seigneurs*).

What does all this mean for the economics profession? On the surface, the findings and conclusions of this book obviously suggest the need for a more careful approach to national accounting, keeping in mind what one really wants to measure – actual production of goods and services, as the textbooks tell us GDP should measure, or incomes out of asset generation and trade, which have nothing to do with real production.

At a deeper level, however, FGDP allows economists to synchronize theoretical and policy stances that are often at odds. A prime example is Paul Krugman, neoclassical in his academic work and publications, but progressive (or liberal, in the American sense of the word) in his widely read policy comments via both blog ("Conscience of a Liberal") and *New York Times* column. A large part of the economics establishment likewise found itself deploying "Keynesian" policies during the crisis without accepting Keynesian theory,[1] which is schizophrenic within the discipline, and confusing to outsiders, both policy makers and ordinary citizens. This is due to GDP showing one thing, and other measures, such as the unemployment rate, showing another.

Spiegler and Milberg (2011) discuss the shallow level of the debate over the state of economics following the financial crisis, referring to proposals for changing economic theory in light of its recent failure to predict or even explain the crisis. They describe three categories of such reform ideas as "Do nothing," "Add finance and stir," and "Add complexity and institutions," but recommend a fourth, deeper approach to reorienting economics, which they call "Connect economics to the economy," involving a "reconsideration of the ontological foundations of economic thought" (33).

This book has made the case for a similar debate on the measurement of economic activity. Perhaps it is not that Keynesian economics is a dead end (Sargent, 1977), but rather that the world has changed drastically since the 1970s, while GDP is a concept dating as far back as 1934 (and its politically contingent nature all the way back to the seventeenth century). The rise of finance after the collapse of the Bretton-Woods system changed the nature of advanced economies, with GDP stretched over the years to try to fit these new realities. In the process, however, measurement went astray by allowing the illusory nature of the FIRE sectors into the world of production. Perhaps the principles of aggregate demand still hold, and can rise out of the ashes, if we put out the FIRE.

Notes

1 Foley (2014) provides a clear discussion of Keynesian vs. Bastard Keynesian theories (such as New Keynesian economics).

References

Akritidis, L. (2007). Improving the measurement of banking services in the UK National Accounts, *Economic & Labour Market Review*, 1(5), May.

Albin, P. S. (1998). *Barriers and Bounds to Rationality*. Princeton, NJ: Princeton University Press.

Arcand, J. L., Berkes, E., and Panizza, U. (2012). *Too Much Finance?* IMF Working Paper WP/12/161, June.

Arrighi, G. (2010). *The Long Twentieth Century: Money, Power and the Origins of our Times*. London and New York: Verso.

Assa, J. (2012). Financialization and its consequences: the OECD experience, *Finance Research*, 1(1), January.

Ball, L. M., Leigh, D., and Loungani, P. (2013). *Okun's Law: Fit at Fifty?* NBER Working Paper 18668, January.

Baltensperger, E. and Jordan, T. J. (1997). Seigniorage, banking, and the optimal quantity of money, *Journal of Banking & Finance*, 21(6): 781–796.

Basu, D. and Foley, D. K. (2013). Dynamics of output and employment in the US economy, *Cambridge Journal of Economics*, 37(5): 1077–1106.

Bos, F. (1992). *The History of National Accounting*. Central Bureau of Statistics, the Netherlands, National Accounts Research Division.

—— (2006). *The National Accounts as a Tool for Analysis and Policy; Past, Present and Future*. PhD dissertation at the University of Twente, Netherlands.

British Academy (2009). *Letter to Her Majesty the Queen*, 22 July, British Academy website, www.britac.ac.uk/news/newsrelease-economy.cfm

Bureau of Economic Analysis (BEA) (2014). The Use of Commodities by Industries, Before Redefinitions (Producers' Prices), *Input–Output Accounts Data,* www.bea.gov/industry/io_annual.htm, accessed October 10, 2014.

Bureau of Economic Analysis (BEA) (2014). *Measuring the Economy: A Primer on GDP and the National Income and Product Accounts*, October.

Bureau of Labor Statistics (BLS) website. www.bls.gov, accessed July 30, 2013.

Butterfield, H. (1931). *The Whig Interpretation of History*. London: W. W. Norton and Company.

Carson, C. S. (1975). The history of the United States national income and product accounts: The development of an analytical tool, *Review of Income and Wealth*, 21(2): 153–181.

Cazes, S., Verick, S., and Al-Hussami, F. (2012). *Diverging Trends in Unemployment in the United States and Europe: Evidence from Okun's Law and the Global Financial Crisis*, Employment Working Papers, ILO.

Chen, P. (2010) *Economic Complexity and Equilibrium Illusion: Essays on Market Instability and Macro Vitality*. London: Routledge.

Christophers, B. (2011). Making finance productive, *Economy and Society*, 40(1), February: 112–140.

Colander, D. (2014). Gross output: A new revolutionary way to confuse students about measuring the economy, *Eastern Economic Journal*, 40: 451–455.

Crowley, P. and Hallet, A. H. (2014). *Volatility Transfers between Cycles: A Theory of Why the "Great Moderation" Was More Mirage than Moderation*, Bank of Finland Research Discussion Papers, 23.

Deane, P. (1955). The implications of early national income estimates for the measurement of long-term economic growth in the United Kingdom, *Economic Development and Cultural Change*, 4(1), Part 1 (October): 3–38.

Desai, R. (2013). *Geopolitical Economy: After US Hegemony, Globalization and Empire*. London: Pluto Press.

—— (2015). Look back in hope? Reassessing Fordism today. In K. Van der Pijl (Ed.), *The International Political Economy of Production*. Cheltenham: Edward Elgar.

dos Santos, P. (2009). On the content of banking in contemporary capitalism, *Historical Materialism*, 17: 1–34.

Economist Intelligence Unit (2013). *New Data Reshape Picture of US Economy.* August 1.

Eisner, R. (1988). Extended accounts for national income and product, *Journal of Economic Literature*, 26(4): 1611–1684.

Epstein, G. (2001). *Financialization, Rentier Interests, and Central Bank Policy*, Manuscript, Department of Economics, University of Massachusetts, Amherst, MA, December.

Federal Reserve Bank of St. Louis (2014). *Velocity of M2 Money Stock*, https://fred.stlouisfed.org/data/M2V.txt, accessed June 11, 2016.

Fisher, I. (1911). *The Purchasing Power of Money*.New York: The Macmillan Company.

Fleurbaey, M. and Blanchet, D. (2013). *Beyond GDP*. Oxford University Press.

Foley, D. K. (1998). An Interview with Wassily Leontief, *Macroeconomic Dynamics*, 2(01), March: 116–140.

—— (2014). *Varieties of Keynesianism*, Schwartz Center for Economic Policy Analysis, The New School, Working Paper 2014-4.

Freeman, R. (2010). It's financialization! *International Labour Review*, 149(2): 163–183.

Gali, J. and Gambetti, L. (2009). On the sources of the Great Moderation, *American Economic Journal: Macroeconomics*, 1(1): 26–57.

Godley, W. (2000). *Drowning in Debt*, The Levy Economics Institute Policy Note 2000/6.

—— (2001). The developing recession in the United States, *BNL Quarterly Review*, 54(219), December: 417–425.

Godley, W. and Wray, L. R. (1999). *Can Goldilocks Survive?* The Levy Economics Institute Policy Note 1999/4.
Gordon, R. J. (2010). Okun's Law and productivity innovation, *American Economic Review: Papers & Proceedings*, 100(2): 11–15.
Haldane, A. (2010). What is the contribution of the financial sector: Miracle or mirage? *In The Future of Finance: The LSE Report*, London School of Economics and Political Science.
Herndon, T., Ash, M. and Pollin, R. (2014). Does high public debt consistently stifle economic growth? A critique of Reinhart and Rogoff, *Cambridge Journal of Economics*, 38(2): 257–250.
Higgins, B. (1978). Velocity: Money's second dimension, *Economic Review*, June.
Hobsbawm, E. (1996). *The Age of Revolution: 1789–1848*. New York: First Vintage Books.
Huffington Post (2010). Goldman Sachs CEO Lloyd Blankfein: Our employees are among the most productive in the world, March 18.
Kedrosky, P. and Stangler, D. (2011). *Financialization and Its Entrepreneurial Consequences*, Kauffman Foundation Research Series: Firm Formation and Economic Growth, March.
Kendrick, J. (1970). The historical development of national accounts, *History of Political Economy*, 2: 284–315.
Keynes, J. M. (1936 [1964]). *The General Theory of Employment, Interest and Money*. New York: Harcourt, Brace and World.
—— (1940). *How to Pay for the War*. New York: Harcourt, Brace & Co.
Kim, C.-J. and Nelson, C. R. (1999). Has the U.S. economy become more stable? A Bayesian approach based on a Markov-switching model of the business cycle, *The Review of Economics and Statistics*, 81(4) (November): 608–616.
Knotek, E. S. (2007). How useful is Okun's Law?, *Economic Review*, Federal Reserve Bank of Kansas City, Fourth Quarter, pp. 73–103.
Krippner, G. (2005). The financialization of the American economy, *Socio-Economic Review*, May, 3(2): 173–208.
Krugman, P. (2013). The Excel depression, *New York Times*, April 18.
Landefeld, J. S., Seskin, E. P., and Fraumeni, B. M. (2008). Taking the pulse of the economy: Measuring GDP, *Journal of Economic Perspectives*, 22(2), Spring.
Lee, P. (2012). *Balancing the Three Approaches to Measuring Gross Domestic Product*, Office for National Statistics, July 31.
Marx, K. (1845). *Theses on Feuerbach, # 11*. www.marxists.org/archive/marx/works/1845/theses/theses.htm, accessed July 31, 2013.
—— (1867 [1992]). *Capital*, Volume I. Penguin Classics; reprint edition, May 5.
Mitra-Kahn, B. H. (2011). *Redefining the Economy: How the "Economy" Was Invented in 1620, and Has Been Redefined Ever Since*. PhD dissertation, City University London, Department of Economics.
Modelski, G. (1978). The long cycle of global politics and the nation-state. *Comparative Studies in Society and History*, 20: 214–235.
O'Brien, E. S. (1998). *Contested Accounts: The Evolution of the Meaning and Measurement of National Income*. PhD dissertation, University of Notre

Dame, ProQuest, UMI Dissertations Publishing. 9823958. (Advisor: Mirowski, Philip E.)

Organisation for Economic Cooperation and Development (OECD) (2014). *Glossary of Statistical Terms*, http://stats.oecd.org/glossary/, accessed May 27, 2016.

——STANdatabase,https://stats.oecd.org/Index.aspx?DataSetCode=STAN08BIS, accessed November 13, 2014.

Oulton, N. (2013). *Has the Growth of Real GDP in the UK Been Overstated because of Mis-Measurement of Banking Output?* Centre for Economic Performance, Occasional Paper #33, January.

Palley, T. I. (2002). Economic contradictions coming home to roost? Does the U.S. economy face a long-term aggregate demand generation problem? *Journal of Post Keynesian Economics*, Fall, 25(1): 9–32.

—— (2007). *Financialization: What It Is and Why It Matters*, The Levy Economics Institute, Washington, DC, Working Paper No. 525, December.

Pressman, S. and Scott, R. (2009). Consumer debt and the measurement of poverty and inequality in the US, *Review of Social Economy*, 67(2): 127–148.

Pyatt, F. G. and Roe, A. (1977). *Social Accounting for Development Planning with Special Reference to Sri Lanka*. Cambridge and New York: Cambridge University Press.

Reinhart, C. and Rogoff, K. S. (2010). Growth in a time of debt, *American Economic Review: Papers & Proceedings*, 100, May: 573–578.

Rosnick, D. and Baker, D. (2011). *When Numbers Don't Add Up: The Statistical Discrepancy in GDP Accounts*, Center for Economic and Policy Research, August.

Rosser, B. R. Jr., Gallegati, M., and Palestrini, A. (2011). The period of financial distress in speculative markets: Interacting heterogeneous agents and financial constraints, *Macroeconomic Dynamics*, 15(01), February: 60–79.

Shaikh, A. and Tonak, E. (1994). *Measuring the Wealth of Nations: The Political Economy of National Accounts*. Cambridge University Press.

Skousen, M. (1990). *The Structure of Production*. New York University Press.

Spiegler, P. and Milberg, W. (2011). *Methodenstreit 2011? Historical Perspective on the Contemporary Debate over How to Reform Economics*, The New School for Social Research, Department of Economics Working Paper 06/2011, October.

Stiglitz, J. E., Sen, A., and Fitoussi, J. P. (2010). *Mismeasuring Our Lives: Why GDP Doesn't Add Up*. New York: The New Press.

—— (2009). *Report by the Commission on the Measurement of Economic Performance and Social Progress*, available from www.stiglitz-sen-fitoussi.fr

Stockhammer, E. (2004). Financialization and the slowdown of accumulation, *Cambridge Journal of Economics*, 28(5): 719–741.

Stone, R. (1978). *Keynes, Political Arithmetic and Econometrics*, Keynes Lecture in Economics, Proceedings of the British Academy.

—— (1984). *The Accounts of Society*. Nobel Memorial Lecture, December 8, Cambridge.

Studenski, P. (1958). *The Income of Nations*. New York University Press.

The Economist (2013). Boundary problems: America has changed the way it measured GDP. August 3.

Thoma, M. (2005). Explaining the discrepancy between GDP and GDP with non-defense related government consumption, *Economist's View*, August 26.

Tily, G. (2009). John Maynard Keynes and the development of national accounts in Britain, 1895–1941, *Review of Income and Wealth*, 2: 331–359.

United Nations (1968). *A System of National Accounts*. Department of Economic and Social Affairs, Series F. No. 2 Rev. 3, New York.

——(1993). *System of National Accounts 2008*. No. E.08.XVII.29, Brussels/ Luxembourg, New York, Paris, Washington, DC.

——(2009). *System of National Accounts 2008*. No. E.08.XVII.29, New York.

United Nations Main Aggregates and Detailed Tables (MADT) database, http:// unstats.un.org/unsd/nationalaccount/madt.asp, accessed May 28, 2014.

United Nations Statistics Division. UN Data Portal, http://data.un.org/, accessed May 13, 2013.

United Nations European Commission, International Monetary Fund, Organisation for Economic Co-operation and Development, and World Bank (2003). Integrated Environmental and Economic Accounting 2003, *Studies in Methods, Handbook of National Accounting*.

Vanoli, A. (2005). *A History of National Accounting*. Amsterdam: IOS.

——(2008). History of national accounting. Entry in *The New Palgrave Dictionary of Economics*, Second Edition, edited by Steven N. Durlauf and Lawrence E. Blume.

Yeldan, A. (2000). *The Impact of Financial Liberalization and the Rise of Financial Rents on Income Inequality: The Case of Turkey*, UNU/WIDER Working Paper No. 206, November.

Index

(Figures indexed in **bold** and Tables in *italic*)

For Product Safety Concerns and Information please contact our EU representative GPSR@taylorandfrancis.com Taylor & Francis Verlag GmbH, Kaufingerstraße 24, 80331 München, Germany